# Facing Up To The Music

# Facing Up To The Music

## A Search for Truth In the Music We Listen To

## Jack R. Christianson

© 1988 Covenant Publishers, Inc.
All Rights Reserved
Printed in the United States of America
Library of Congress Catalog Number 88–063878
Jack R. Christianson
Facing Up to the Music
Printed March 1989
ISBN 1–555–03–074–2

# Dedication

To Melanie who worked endless hours on this project
and who gave me the inspiration to
keep trying.

# Contents

# Acknowledgments

No book is the sole project of the author. Many people are required to make a successful publication. Among these I especially wish to thank are Janet Thomas for her editing skills which have made me a better writer and Lew Kofford for his patience and willingness to take a chance with my work.

**One**

# Never Fearing Truth

The air had a smell of pine and a mixture of wild flowers. The pleasant rolling sound of a nearby stream greeted my ears as I walked along the grey and white gravel path enjoying the various aromas and sounds of the forest. I felt the familiar excitement of speaking at a youth conference come in the form of sweaty palms and butterflies in the pit of my stomach. For some unknown reason I was particularly nervous as I walked along the dimly lit path. During the preceding years I had spoken on music and its effects on our actions, feelings, thoughts, and spirituality hundreds of times, so it was a little confusing to be so nervous. The fireside was scheduled late and the young people were very tired and a lecture on a topic as sensitive as music would be difficult. The fact that so many would be coming with pre-conceived biases and walls of defense set up had apparently put me a little on edge. The influence of the Spirit was needed, desperately needed, for, "if ye receive not the Spirit ye shall not teach," (D&C 42:14). By having the Spirit, these walls could be broken down.

I tried to concentrate on the sweet smells and sounds of the forest as I walked in hopes of relaxing somewhat. I glanced at my watch but couldn't see the time because the tall pine trees hanging over the path blocked most of the moonlight. I held my right arm in the air in hopes that one of the dim path lights would aid me. It did. The time to begin the fireside was not far away, so I picked up my pace and hurried toward the main conference gathering place.

As I approached the arena, stereo cassette player and briefcase in hand, I noticed four young men standing under a path light, listening intensely to some music. It wasn't difficult to tell what type of music they were playing as the heavy metal sounds screamed out through the night air. Chuckling to myself I thought, "Man, these guys are really getting prepared spiritually to hear me speak." Putting my briefcase and stereo under one arm I headed towards them hoping to shake hands and give them a little bit of a hard time all in fun.

As I approached, the boy holding the industrial-sized stereo on his shoulder set it down and started walking towards me. How do I describe him? He was not very tall, maybe 5' 5" or 6" at the most. His hair was, well, unique. The style wasn't necessarily that of a "rocker," "punker," "new waver," or country western. It was a conglomerate of three or four styles. Dangling from his left ear was an earring. He wore a black leather jacket with a small chain over one shoulder. Both wrists were circled with spiked wristbands. His black t-shirt bore the logo of a heavy metal band that I assumed he had bought at one of their concerts.

As the distance between us narrowed I smiled, said hello, and stretched out my hand to shake his. Instead of shaking hands he completely surprised me by slapping my hand to the side and poking me in the center of the chest with his right forefinger. As his finger was pressing against my tie, he began to shake his rear end back and forth while asking me a startling question. "Are you the chump that's going to tell us all our rock 'n' roll music is bad and if we listen to heavy metal we're all going to hell?"

What could I say? It wasn't clear to me if he was serious or if he had just beat me to the punch and was giving me a hard time, in jest, before I could do it to him. It took me by surprise.

I told him, "Yeah, I'm the speaker, and I'm speaking on music, but I'm not going to tell you what I think is good and bad in music. I'd like to show you how to choose appropriately and how music affects your actions, feelings, thoughts, and spirituality and then let you make your own decisions about what you will or will not listen to."

Without waiting for more he took aim again with his finger and poked me in the chest a second time. Again with his finger on my tie, he asked basically the same question, "Listen Mr. Chump, are you going to tell us all our heavy metal is bad and if we listen to rock 'n' roll we're all going to hell?"

By this time I was trying to suppress my anger because I was beginning to realize he wasn't just kidding around. I started to shake and could feel the tips of my ears getting hot.

I responded, "I'm only going to tell you two things, partner. Number one, please don't touch me again, and number two, please don't call me chump, because you are really starting to irritate me."

I had no sooner said those words when, Bam! his finger made contact with my chest a third time. With somewhat of a raised voice he said, "If you tell me my heavy metal music or my rock 'n' roll is bad, I'll get up and I'll leave your discussion." In my mind, I reasoned, "If that's all it takes, he is as good as gone!"

He walked away somewhat jokingly saying, "I'll leave! I'll leave!" I couldn't resist, so I yelled back, while motioning towards him with the back of my hand, "Go ahead and leave, son. Go ahead and leave!"

When I finally reached the location where the fireside was to be held, I prayed desperately for the Spirit to be with me and tried to gather my thoughts after my unforgettable encounter in the forest. When I reached the pulpit and looked at the audience, there sat my young "friend" with all his little buddies. They were on the second row directly in front of where I had to stand and speak for the next hour and a half. I tried to ignore them but, it was a little difficult to do with each of them sitting with folded arms and eyes glaring the message, "Go ahead chump, just try and tell us anything is wrong with our music. Try and teach us or make us change!"

I had been speaking for about 45 minutes when the time for me to talk about learning how to choose arrived. I quoted some verses from the seventh chapter of Moroni. While doing so, a phrase from the film, "Man's Search for Happiness," raced into my mind. "Only if you are unafraid of truth will you ever find it." I had heard that phrase many times in the past and had even used it in several of my talks. But never before had it come into my mind with such force. That seemed to be the answer. How would anyone ever find truth if they feared it?

With this thought, I quoted the phrase with emphasis and then did something I had never done before or since. I looked directly at the young man and repeated the phrase. "Only if you are unafraid of truth will you ever find it." I wanted to call him a chump but didn't. Not taking my eyes off of him I said, "Young man, you are afraid of the truth, and until you have the courage to face it and not fear it, it will elude you forever!"

He glared back as if to say, "How dare you say that to me."

I glared right back saying to myself, "How dare I say that?" He and I were both shocked.

After the bold stares, he bowed his head in silence and did not look up at me again for the remainder of the talk. Now the audience was captivated! You could have heard a pin drop. My head felt hot as I felt the pressure of their eyes.

The first of a series of questions I presented pierced the tense silence. "Young people, are you afraid of truth? Does it embarrass you, or are you ashamed to be a member of the church of Jesus Christ? Are you uncomfortable with the fact that you are supposed to live life differently than the rest of the world? Does it bother you to be identified with cleanliness, goodness, and virtue? Do you struggle with the standard that says you are not to be involved in immorality, drugs, or alcohol like so many in the world? Truth will require sacrifice and may be difficult on the ego. Do you have the courage it takes to live truth?"

Most in attendance, including myself, were stunned with the straight forwardness of my questioning. These deep, penetrating questions led us into an exciting discussion about the values and difficulties associated with finding and living truth.

We quoted the words of the Apostle Peter from 2 Peter 2:1-2 concerning false teachers in the last days teaching that "the way of truth shall be evil spoken of." We determined that it would not be easy. We talked of the change that may come about as a result of truth and how change is often difficult and requires stretching. Leaving the comfort zone is very difficult. But the Savior taught that by knowing and living the truth, we would actually find freedom. (See John 8:32). This freedom paves the way for us to have the Spirit and rid ourselves of the shackles of deception. "For the Spirit speaketh the truth and lieth not. Wherefore, it speaketh of things as they really are, and of things as they really will be," (Jacob 4:13).

As our discussion on truth ended and we headed back to the assigned topic of music and how it affects us, I noticed that the young man on the second row still had his head down and would not look at me. Inside I hoped I had not offended him but was certain I had. I felt like Nephi talking to Laman and Lemuel. They complained that he had spoken hard things to them, but he responded, "I knew that I had spoken hard things against the wicked, according to the truth; . . . wherefore, the guilty taketh the truth to be hard, for it cutteth them to the very center," (1Nephi16:2). I wasn't sure he had been cut to the "very center" but I knew something was going on inside him. The talk ended on a very positive note, yet, he still refused to look at me.

After the meeting was over, I stood in front of the pulpit talking and shaking hands with some of the youth and their leaders. It wasn't long before I noticed the young man from the second row standing in line waiting, I thought, to shake my hand and talk. When he reached the front of the line, he raised his finger, the same one he had poked me in the chest with, and started waving it in my face. This time he didn't touch me but made his feelings very well known. "I want to talk with you, mister! Alone!"

"Great, " I thought. "He probably wants to kill me after embarrassing him in front of all his friends."

We arranged for a time the following morning just before breakfast. I knew it would be light and there would be lots of people around. He left. I went on shaking hands.

It wasn't too long before I left the building and headed for my sleeping quarters about a half-a-mile away through the trees. It was very pleasant to walk through the pines again and smell the familiar smells that had greeted me a few hours earlier. The path was once again lit by the dim path lights and a faint moon was trying to make its way through a few scattered late night clouds.

I hadn't gone far when I noticed someone standing behind a tree watching me. My heart began to pound and my palms to sweat when I recognized the haircut. It was my young "friend."

"Maybe he really is going to kill me," I thought, as he walked slowly in my direction.

Before either of us spoke, my mind began to do crazy things. I started thinking of all the things I would do if he tried anything tricky. I felt a little like Thomas Magnum in a tight situation. My heart felt like it was in my throat. It was pounding with anticipation as he approached.

"Brother Christianson, could I have a few minutes of your time before you go to bed?" His voice was soft now and subdued. His eyes did not look anywhere but at his shoes. "I'm afraid if I wait until morning I won't have the courage to talk to you."

"Sure," I said, knowing he could probably detect my nervousness by the shakiness of my voice. "Before we talk, could I have two things from you first?"

"Yeah, I guess so."

"First of all, what's your name?"

"Jim," he said, almost muffling his voice. "Could we find a place to sit down? This might take a while." Little did I know then, as we walked back down the lighted path towards the kitchen area, just how long it would be. Our talk lasted almost three complete hours. We spotted a large piece of cement in a small bunch of trees just off the path. It was right below a light, so I felt pretty safe.

"Well, Jim, the second thing I'd like to ask is for your forgiveness. Will you please forgive me for embarrassing you in front of all your friends?"

"Maybe I needed it," he answered rudely, his eyes now glaring at me, no longer looking at his shoes.

"Well, excuse me!" I thought, as I glared right back. I sat on the cement, somewhat uncomfortable at his Dr. Jeckle and Mister Hyde behavior.

The silence was killing me as we sat not knowing what to say about what had just happened. So mustering up some courage, I asked, "What do you mean you needed it?" He didn't hesitate with his reply.

"Tonight, for the first time in my life, I asked myself if I were afraid of truth."

"What did you find out," I asked somewhat sarcastically.

"I'm terrified!" he cried. His head sagged again towards the ground. He tried to stop the tears with the back of his hand, but it was too late. They were already on their way off the end of his nose and chin and had dripped onto the cement block.

"If I live the truth, Brother Christianson, I have to give up every one of my friends, in the Church and out."

"You don't have to give up all of them, do you?" I asked innocently.

"I said all of them!" he said angrily. Again, I was stunned by his sudden change in behavior. Here he was yelling at me through his tears and all I wanted to do was help the poor guy.

"Every one of my friends is involved in drugs or alcohol or both." He glanced at me briefly with a pained look in his eye and then hid his face behind his arm that was wrapped around his knee.

"Are you involved, Jim?" Again the tears started to flow as he explained to me about his involvement. I cried and my heart ached as I listened to his sad story.

After we discussed his problems concerning drugs and alcohol, we launched into another deep discussion. Jim said, "After listening to you speak tonight, if I live the truth, I think I have to get rid of all my music."

"Now wait a minute, Slick," I said jokingly. "I never told you to get rid of all your music." Apparently that's all it took to set him off again.

He yelled, "I said I have to get rid of all of it!"

"Go ahead, burn the whole pile you ornery little beggar!" I thought to myself as I contemplated how to ask him the next question without setting him off again. "Why do you have to get rid of all of it?"

He didn't even flinch with his answer. "Because my music makes me feel exactly the way I want to feel."

"How's that?"

"Angry!"

"Why?"

"Because I hate my dad!" With this admission, his lower lip started to quiver and the tears began once more.

We both sat in silence under the light while he gained his composure. The various sounds and smells of the crisp mountain air seemed to bring courage and comfort as we began a lengthy discussion concerning the many difficulties of his home life. As we discussed the situation in his home, too personal to write about, he surprised me once more with a penetrating question. His voice was shaky and with a deliberate hesitancy he asked, "Would you be my dad?"

"Yeah, . . . uh . . . I guess so. What do you mean by that?" I asked before my mind had an opportunity to contemplate all that being the father of a troubled 14-year-old boy would entail.

"I don't want to come and live with you or anything like that," he said, bringing much relief to my heart. "I just want you to call me on the phone or come and see me when you come this way again. I guess I just want you to help me live the truth. Can you do that?" he pleaded, while his eyes looked at me like one of my own children asking for a special favor.

"Sure Jim. I'd be honored to help any way that I can."

By the time we had discussed Jim's family problems the night had moved into the early morning hours. I was extremely tired and definitely ready for bed, but Jim still needed to talk.

"Before you go to bed, Brother Christianson, I have one more thing to tell you. If I live the truth, I think I have to go and talk to my bishop. Are you a bishop?" he asked, with hope in his voice.

"Yes, but I'm not your bishop," I answered quickly.

He was quick to interject, "You see, my bishop knows my mom, and I know if I go to him she'll find out everything. How about if I tell you everything, and it'll be our little secret?"

"I wish it were that easy. You can tell me if you want, but you still have to talk to your own bishop."

He looked off into the trees and then slowly turned his head towards me. By the look on his face it was obvious an idea was churning in his mind.

"How about if I tell you everything I've done and then you tell me if I need to go or not, and if I don't I won't? Sound like a deal?"

"That's fine, but you'll have to hurry because I can hardly keep my eyes open," I said realizing I was in for quite a story.

Again we discussed items too personal to write about. He didn't leave out anything as far as I could tell. I sat on the rock in wonderment trying to imagine how a 14-year-old boy could have been involved so deeply in so many things of the world. When he finished, he very confidently asked, "Well, what do you think? Do you think I ought to go talk with my bishop or not?"

I cleared my throat and weakly said, "Hurry!" He said he would soon but would commit to nothing definite.

By this time I was so tired I could hardly keep my eyes open. I stood up from the rock, swatted him affectionately with my right hand on the shoulder, and let him know we'd have to finish in the morning.

I started to walk away and had only walked 15 or 20 paces when I received the greatest shock of the evening. "Brother Christianson," he called out, "Would you think it was crazy if I gave you a hug?"

I turned and saw his unusual haircut silhouetted in the light behind the rock. The shadows hid his face, but I could tell he was serious.

"Get over here," I lovingly commanded as I motioned for him to come to me.

What followed next I have never been able to forget or erase from my memory. He put his arms around me and rested his head on my chest and hugged me tightly as if he were my own child. We both sobbed as we stood there on the path. I tried to pat him on the head, but it was a little difficult getting my hand to rub smoothly over the top of his head because of his hairstyle.

He only wanted to know three simple things: Can I be forgiven? Is it all really worth it? Do you promise to help me live truth? As I fought the tears and the large lump in my throat, all I could muster was one feeble "yes" to each question. We walked arm in arm for a few steps down the path and made some very special promises to one another concerning truth. We both realized then how difficult it would be to find and live truth when so many were mocking and fearing it.

The now familiar sounds and smells of that forest almost seemed to communicate their agreement. Truth would require change and would be a very difficult and life-long process. Jim had a long way to go in his quest but had overcome one of the major hurdles. He was learning not to fear it. He was willing, for the time being, to pay whatever price was necessary.

The following morning after breakfast I prepared to leave the mountain resort and head back to Salt Lake City. As I climbed into the car and sat down on the sun-heated seat I heard the sound of music and laughter filter through the trees. The thought hit me that no one at the conference but myself and Jim was aware of what had taken place on a cement block adjacent to the pathway in a small bunch of trees.

As I asked myself about the reality of Jim keeping his commitment to live the truth, I saw him running towards the car. I closed the door and rolled down the window.

"You promised me you'd help me live truth and that you'd call and write me," he said as he stood beside the car with his thumbs hooked inside the front pockets of his jeans.

"Yes, I did, my friend, and I will." Before rolling up the window I stretched out my arm and shook his hand. "I'll look forward to hearing from you real soon, buddy." He acknowledged the statement with a nod of his head and stood watching as I drove out of sight.

The air conditioning felt cool and refreshing as it blew against my bare face and arms. As I rode along the winding road that made its way out of the mountains towards the airport I thought of Jim and what we had just experienced. For some reason I also thought of Lehi and his vision of the great and spacious building. "And great was the multitude that did enter into that strange building. And after they did enter into that building they did point the finger of scorn at me and those that were partaking of the fruit also; but we heeded them not," (I Nephi 8:33). I came to the realization that many would mock and seek to destroy Jim's attempt to live the truth, not only concerning music, but also in every other area of his life.

I have not seen Jim since that afternoon. We have communicated by mail, and he has given permission to share this story. His courage to face the truth and try to live it has given me great courage and a desire to follow his example.

The purpose of this book is not to tear down rock 'n' roll or any other type of music. It is to educate and edify the reader. Much has been written in recent years about the many challenges associated with contemporary music, its artists and lifestyles. News articles, firesides and lectures on the subject have become commonplace. It is quite simple to find something wrong with almost anything if you look hard or long enough. That is not my objective. The objective is to teach the truth as I understand it and encourage the reader to choose for himself. However, when choosing for ourselves and exercising agency, we must remember that responsibility for those choices, good or bad, becomes vital. Each individual must accept and live with the consequences of their decisions and choices. One cannot escape it.

Just before Jesus was put to death he was asked of Pilate, "What is truth?" This question was Pilate's response to Jesus' statement, "To this end was I born, and for this cause came I into the world, that I should bear witness unto the truth. Everyone that is of the truth heareth my voice," (John 18:37).

Jesus answered nothing on this occasion. Centuries later, however, he gave a thought-provoking answer to the Prophet Joseph Smith. "And truth is a knowledge of things as they are, and as they were, and as they are to come," (D&C 93:24). Truth about music, videos, or anything else in life is the same yesterday, today, and forever. It can be found. It is available to all who do not fear it.

Two

# Our Lives And Music

Sometime ago while hunting deer with my father in the mountains of central Utah, I had an experience that helped me better understand the pervasive and encompassing nature of music. We hiked to the top of a rather high knoll. When we reached our predetermined destination, we found a comfortable hiding spot under a tall bushy pine tree and awaited for the arrival of our winter dinner. It was a beautiful sight to sit and watch the mountain below us as well as the vast mountain range surrounding our secluded perch. We were surrounded by miles and miles of tree-covered hills with meadows of sagebrush and tall grass spotting each ravine and gully.

There I sat, alone with my dad, exchanging whispered conversation, drinking ice cold water from a canteen, and eating apples and miniature Hershey chocolate bars. It was wonderful! It was the first time we had hunted together for several years, and neither of us was too interested in killing a deer. We simply wanted to be together and enjoy the beauty and wonder of being in the mountains and away from the pressures of the valley.

As the sun fought to make its way over a group of early morning clouds, we enjoyed each other's company and the bliss of that moment. Without warning, the bliss was interrupted as the soft eastern wind brought with it, of all things, the sound of an electric guitar. It became louder and louder with each second. It wasn't long before we spied the source of the piercing rhythms bouncing their way up the mountainside. A would-be hunter in a fairly late model four-wheel drive pickup, evidently with an outrageous sound system, was enjoying his music at an extremely high volume level. When he reached the top of the knoll below us, he stopped the truck, opened the door, and stepped out. I couldn't believe it! The speakers attached to the door were sending screams of music across the valleys and dells with little respect for the two hunters sitting beneath the pine tree. If there had been any deer in the immediate area, they were now well on their way to a new and more quiet hiding place. When the guy finally turned off his stereo system, I turned to my dad and said, "See dad, what have I been telling you? Music is everywhere! We can't even get away from it in the tops of the mountains!"

Without answering, he raised his rifle to his shoulder and clicked a shell into the chamber. I sat watching as he aimed his rifle at the cab of the truck. "Well, I can get away from it, son" he said, chuckling under his breath.

"No, dad!" I laughed, while reaching for the barrel of his gun with my hand. He ejected the shell out of the chamber, looked at me, and we both started to laugh. "I guess you're right son. I guess some people just can't live without it, can they?"

Obviously we didn't get a deer, but we both learned something about music. We learned that just about everywhere we go, from the dentist's office, to the supermarket, to the athletic fields, to being put on hold on the telephone, to the tops of the mountains, music is all around us.

Very few lives are not affected profoundly by music. Regardless of what we choose to listen to or watch, whether it be rock, jazz, classical, country western, new wave, punk, soul, reggae, heavy metal, devotional, religious, or elevator music, in many instances our actions, feelings, thoughts, hairstyles, clothing, and spirituality are affected in one way or another by our musical or visual diet.

Volumes have been written about music. Armies have been motivated by it; teenagers camp for days to purchase tickets to hear it; athletic events would often be dry without it; movies and TV have come alive because of it; air waves buzz with it; prophets, as well as their followers, sing praises to God through it; and unfortunately many families have been and are becoming divided or disrupted by it.

Music is one of the most powerful stimuli known among the human senses. A person does not have to know a whole lot about the music to enjoy it. Music, like food, can be enjoyed immensely without a knowledge of how it was prepared or packaged. Perhaps this is why so many people, young and old alike, are involved so deeply in music. It is a chance to fantasize, to live dreams through the successes and lives of others. By immersing ourselves in music, it is possible to escape from the many pressures and stressful situations created by our modern society.

Music has been one of the most common expressions of man's feelings since the beginning of human history. Man has always sung. Many of the great thinkers of antiquity emphasized the powerful effect of music upon the character of man. Confucius, Plato, Aristotle, and many, many others were convinced that music molded character. Perhaps the old axiom, "As in music, so in life," is more of a truism than any of us have ever realized.

For civilized man, music, in many instances, has become an international language. Feelings can be communicated by music that words simply cannot express. Though the words may be in different languages, the music communicates to the soul. Perhaps this is why the First Presidency of The Church of Jesus Christ of Latter-day Saints stated, "Through music man's ability to express himself extends beyond the limits of the spoken language in both subtlety and power. Music can be used to both exalt and inspire or to carry messages of degradation and destruction. It is therefore important that as Latter-day Saints we apply the principles of the gospel and seek the guidance of the Spirit in selecting the music with which we surround ourselves," (Priesthood Bulletin, vol. 9, no. 4, Aug. 1973, p.3).

If we honestly approach the study of the influence of music in our lives, it is impossible to say that music does not affect us in one way or another. Surveys have shown that the average American teenager listens to no less than three to four hours of music each day, (see U.S. News and World Report, Oct. 28, 1985, p. 49).

There are very few of us, in the modern world, that are not affected in some way or that do not hear a number of hours of music daily.

Think for a moment what life would be like if music were to be banned from our society for just 30 days. Could you go for 30 days consecutively without listening to any type of music, whatsoever? At first it may appear to be a simple task, however with some investigation we realize that it would be nearly impossible. Thirty days with no music would mean no shopping at the local supermarket, no visits to the dentist's office, doctor's office, and few rides on elevators. A person could not even get put on hold on the telephone in many locations without listening to music. No music for 30 days would mean no live athletic events, no TV, movies, radio, concerts, dances, parades, very little of anything. In fact we wouldn't even be able to attend school. I challenge any reader to walk down the halls of any high school in America without hearing music. You certainly would not be able to attend church because Section 25:12 of the Doctrine and Covenants reads, "For my soul delighteth in the song of the heart; yea, the song of the righteous is a prayer unto me, and it shall be answered with a blessing upon their heads."

The Lord tells us that "the song of the heart; yea the song of the righteous," is a prayer unto him. One of the major reasons we sing in church, then, is to extend our prayers to our Father in Heaven. We can hardly expect those who go to worship their God not to pray to him in song.

Thirty days without music would be practically impossible. Oh, it might be done with a great deal of work and effort, but for most it would be a very difficult task. After all, what is the first thing many people do when they get up in the morning, especially teenagers? Do they turn on the radio? Some even wake up to a clock radio! The first thing pumped into their systems every day of their lives is music. How can we say that it will not have a profound effect on our actions, feelings, thoughts, and spirit?

Not only is it the first thing we often do in the morning, but many times it is also one of the first things we do when we get into a car of any kind. Almost immediately, after starting the engine, we begin to push buttons and turn knobs until we find the tune we want and then a strange human phenomenon occurs. The windows go up, and we begin to have our own concert inside the car. The person driving begins to tap out the rhythm of the tune on the steering wheel. Sometimes, he even sings into his thumb, posing as a microphone. The person in the passenger seat plays his imaginary drums on the dashboard or his keyboards along the glove compartment. Heads begin to bob like a large bird during a courting ritual and facial expressions, along with sincere and serious singing, tell the story of the type of song being listened to. Some people speed up or slow down or just space out, depending on the kind of music they are digesting.

It is hilarious to pull up beside them and watch as they fantasize themselves into the dream world of being a star. Most of the time these stoplight performers have no idea how they are acting until they look over at someone in another car watching and being entertained. They immediately realize they are making fools of themselves and flip their heads forward in embarrassment and conclude their concert. Some people, however, when they know they have an audience, intensify their level of performance to the enjoyment of all who are watching.

If listening to music is the first thing many people do when they get up in the morning and one of the first things they do when they get into a car, what is the last thing many people do before they go to bed at night? Some people can't even sleep without the narcotic of music. Yet some claim it has no effect upon them. How many parents or brothers or sisters have crept silently into a loved one's room late at night, or early in the morning, to turn off a radio or stereo that was left on because the room's occupant was unable to sleep without it playing?

With this type of powerful influence in our lives, would it not be wise to be cautious when choosing the type of music we listen to or watch? It is important and can be a wonderful, exhilarating form of entertainment. However, if misused, it can become a very degrading or demoralizing activity.

There is little argument that youth entertainment is a lucrative part of a three hundred billion dollar a year leisure activity market, (see *U.S. News and World Report*, Oct. 28, 1985, p. 48).

Studies show that teenagers listen to an estimated 10,500 hours of rock music between the seventh and the twelfth grades. That works out to just 500 hours less than they spend of the twelve years they are in school. Children between ages two and twelve watch an average of 25 hours of television a week, most of that television being accompanied by musical scores, (see *U.S. News and World Report,* Oct. 28, 1985, p. 46).

Because our society lends itself to so much sitting and watching and absorbing rather than participating, it is very easy for contention or strife to arise. Perhaps contention in the home is one of the great tragedies of life. Oft- times, music contributes to that contention. Battle lines are drawn over what is appropriate and what is not. Parents, at times, become enraged with some of the popular music and children feel that their parents' music is old-fashioned and slow. It becomes a contest of wills. Each defends his position of who is right and who is wrong rather than what is right. It has been so in almost every generation. With the rising of tempers it is soon forgotten that just because a person likes the music does not make it appropriate and just because he dislikes it does not make it inappropriate. We may enjoy the feeling of driving a car off a three-hundred-foot cliff. It's probably a real rush all the way to the bottom. However, when the car hits the ground, it is not a good or beneficial experience.

We must never forget that contention, in any form, is not of God. In fact the Savior taught the Nephites in 3 Nephi 11:29 that, "He that hath the spirit of contention is not of me, but is of the devil, who is the father of contention, and he stirreth up the hearts of men to contend with anger, one with another."

Is there contention in your home over music? If there is, for any reason, hopefully the following stories will aid you in understanding the power music can have when used as a tool to dispel contention and, at times, to create it if wisdom is not used. Wisdom becomes vital when families are in disagreement concerning this sensitive subject. Some good advice is the same as the prophet Jacob, the brother of Nephi, gave. "O be wise; what can I say more?" (Jacob 6:12).

Contention, like so many other things, is a tool of the adversary to destroy individuals and families. There is no worse feeling for me than to be at odds with those I love most. A feeling of darkness prevails. A sickening nausea and emptiness converges upon me. Yet, on the other hand, there is perhaps no greater feeling than to have harmony and peace with loved ones.

I remember a time in my youth when I had a disagreement with my mother. I cried, complained, and even threatened to run away. It was an idle threat, but I threatened to do it, nevertheless. After a few minutes of disagreement, I could stand it no longer. I headed for my bedroom with the intention of slamming the door, getting my jacket, and leaving for good.

As I hurried down the hallway I cried out, "You don't love me anymore! You never let me do anything!" The funny thing is, I don't even remember why we were having the disagreement.

When my mother heard that I thought she didn't love me anymore, she said something that caused chills to run through my body. She commanded, "Young man, you stop right there!" I knew she meant business. She was the type who wouldn't hesitate to chase me down the block, tackle me on the neighbor's lawn, then bring me home. Seldom, if ever, did she wait for my father to return home before taking care of the problem. (In order to appreciate this story, you must realize that I was much more afraid of my mother than almost anyone else alive. Don't get me wrong, she was the greatest, but when she said stop she meant stop! and I knew it.) I stopped and with a quivering voice replied again, "Why should I? You don't love me anymore. You never let me do anything!"

She repeated the same command. "Young man! I said stop right there!" After telling me to stop she brushed by me as if I didn't exist and went into her bedroom. She returned shortly with a suitcase in her hands. After a cold, yet loving look, she walked by me again and entered my room. I stood and watched in utter amazement as she opened the suitcase, pulled out my dresser drawers, and emptied most of my clothes into the suitcase. Without a word she snapped it shut and then peered at me like only a "loving" mother can.

As our eyes met, I could see her true sweetness, but I tried to ignore it. I knew she could sense that I was totally uncomfortable and did not know how to handle such an abrupt action. I mean, after all, I was her sweet, spoiled, baby boy. I had always felt that she thought I was something special. But now I didn't know what to think, and she knew it!

We were still exchanging bold stares when she spoke and nearly broke my heart. "Jackie," she replied, handing me the suitcase, "if you think you can find a better mother somewhere else or one who loves you more than me, go ahead, leave!"

I couldn't believe it. My heart was telling me, "Don't, she loves you can't you see?" But my pride said, "Okay, I'll show her she can't treat me that way." I left.

Where was I to go? The only alternatives were the school, the orchards, my friends, or the horse trailer parked in the field behind our home. I made my way to the trailer, threw my suitcase in, and then climbed in after it.

I remember how terrible it was to be in that place because it appeared and smelled like it hadn't been cleaned in years. But I decided it didn't matter. I would stay there no matter what! My parents were going to learn a real lesson from me.

I didn't anticipate falling asleep but did so shortly after placing myself on one of the wheel wells. I was awakened by the sound of my dog barking and jumping up and down at the side of the trailer.

When I came to my senses I could hear my father calling my name. I quickly tried to quiet the dog before he gave my hiding place away. However, it was too late. In the middle of one of the quieting attempts, I felt the trailer tip to one side and knew the day of reckoning had come! My dad had climbed up on the outside wheel well and was peering down at me like death itself.

Up to that point in my life I wasn't too sure if the Lord really answered prayers, but I'll tell you, I prayed without ceasing for deliverance.

Almost before my prayers had a chance to get out of the trailer, my dad in his deep and somewhat angry voice commanded, "Young man, get out of the trailer, now!" I was petrified, so I pretended that I was still asleep. He gave the same command once more, I continued to pretend, He didn't wait to ask me a third time. Before I knew it, he had reached in with his thick hand and pulled me out of that smelly place and set me on my feet. My hands immediately went to my backside for protection. However, the expected swat never came. Instead, he placed his strong but loving arm around my shoulders and said, "Oh son, I'm so glad I found you. Your mother and I have been worried sick. Won't you come home and eat dinner with us?"

I replied with a sigh of relief and thanksgiving, "Ah . . . yeah, I guess I could."

We walked arm in arm back to the house. As we walked through the door and down the hallway, I could smell the familiar smell of my mother's cooking. When I reached the end of the hallway, I stood at the bottom of the two steps that led into the kitchen. There she stood, her apron smudged with spills, her hair disheveled, her glasses on the end of her nose, and tears in her eyes. She walked over to where I was standing, kneeled down on the floor, and placed her tender hands on my cheeks. This time, as she looked in my eyes, I melted and my pride ran back to the horse trailer. She cried and said softly, "Oh Jackie, will you ever forgive me for being such a terrible mother?"

I fell into her arms and muttered through my tears, "You're the best mother in the whole world!"

As I look back in time and compare the nausea of fighting with the bliss of harmony, my heart aches. Why are we so foolish as to let little insignificant items destroy the beauty of peaceful homes? Why are some of the young people and their parents willing to let the most sacred and important relationships in their lives, those with their families, be marred or damaged for a silly, insignificant record, tape, video, or concert ticket that won't even be popular in a year anyway? Is it really worth it? I think not. Think for a moment—aren't peaceful moments or occasions worth keeping? Aren't they worth more than the $9.99 a music tape may cost? I hope so.

If I could relive the few hours previously described, I can assure each reader that I would do all that was in my power to control the situation and have only the peaceful time and get rid of the contentions. Music does play an important role in controlling or contributing to contentious situations in our daily lives as well as in our homes.

Mick Jagger, the lead singer in the musical group, *The Rolling Stones,* and nicknamed the Lucifer of rock, has commented on the relationship between music and contention in the home. "There's no future in rock 'n' roll. It's only recycled past. Basically, rock 'n' roll isn't protest, and never was. It's only—it promotes interfamilial tension. It used to. Now it can't even do that, because fathers don't ever get outraged with the music. Either they like it, or it sounds similar to what they liked as kids. So rock 'n' roll's gone, that's all gone," (*Newsweek,* April 1982, p. 104). Perhaps this is why some artists have moved into areas, in their performing, that will offend many parents.

Another well-known performer commented: "Our music is intended to broaden the generation gap, to alienate children from their parents and to prepare people for the revolution," (*The Plain Truth,* Sept,. 1980, p. 1).

What are we to believe when some of the best-known performers are so vocal about the fact that much of their music is written for the specific purpose of causing contention in families? It's frightening. In fact, the lead singer of one of the most popular groups declared that he and the other group members "wanted to be the group parents hate." Why? Because then music would be purchased that normally would not be allowed, thus, increasing their financial security.

Money is the name of the game for music promoters. Little thought is given to the effects on the consumer. If a product generates revenue then it is produced. That's a little scary when you consider that listening to music is one of the first things young people do every morning. It is one of the first things they do when they get in a car and one of the last things they do when they go to bed at night, and as we have mentioned so often in this chapter, music pervades the airwaves everywhere they go throughout their daily activities.

Contrast these attitudes with those of President Heber J. Grant.

He described the beautiful power of music and how it can soothe irritated feelings and a contentious spirit. "I recall one incident showing how song has the power to soothe irritated feelings and bring harmony to the hearts of men who are filled with a contentious spirit. It occurred many years ago, and involved a quarrel between two old and faithful brethren who's membership dated back to the days of Nauvoo. They had been through many of the hardships of Nauvoo and had suffered the drivings and persecutions of the Saints, as well as the hardships of pioneering incident to the early settlement of the west. These men had quarreled over some business affairs and finally concluded that they would try to get President John Taylor to help them adjust their difficulties.

"John Taylor was then the President of the Council of the Twelve Apostles. These brethren pledged their word of honor that they would faithfully abide by whatever decision Brother Taylor might render. Like many others, even in these days, they were not willing to accept the conclusions and counsels of their teachers, or bishops, or presidents of stakes, who would have been the authorized persons, in their order, to consult, and which would have been the proper course to pursue, but they must have some higher authority. Having been personally acquainted with President Brigham Young, in the days of Nauvoo, and feeling their importance in their own devotion to the work of the Lord, nothing short of an Apostle's advice would seem to satisfy them.

"Accordingly they called on President Taylor, but did not immediately tell him what their trouble was, but explained that they had seriously quarreled and asked him if he would listen to their story and render his decision. President Taylor willingly consented. But he said: 'Brethren, before I hear your case, I would like very much to sing one of the songs of Zion for you.' Now President Taylor was a very capable singer, and interpreted sweetly and with spirit, our sacred hymns. He sang one of our hymns to the two brethren. Seeing its effect, he remarked that he never heard one of the songs of Zion but that he wanted to listen to one more, and so asked them to listen while he sang another. Of course, they consented. They both seemed to enjoy it; and, having sung the second song, he remarked that he had heard there is luck in odd numbers and so with their consent he would sing still another, which he did. Then, in his jocular way, he remarked: 'Now brethren, I do not want to wear you out, but if you will forgive me, and listen to one more hymn, I promise to stop singing, and will hear your case.'

The story goes that when President Taylor had finished the fourth song, the brethren were melted to tears, got up, shook hands, and asked President Taylor to excuse them for having called upon him, and for taking up his time. They then departed without his even knowing what their difficulties were. President Taylor's singing had reconciled their feelings toward each other. The Spirit of the Lord had entered their hearts, and the hills of difference that rose between them had been leveled and become as nothing. Love and brotherhood had developed in their souls, and the trifles over which they had quarreled, had become of no consequence in their sight. The songs of the heart had filled them with the spirit of reconciliation," (*Improvement Era,* Sept. 1940, p. 52).

In my own home, my wife and I try to dispel the irritating and contentious feelings that can arise while putting children to bed at night by playing beautiful, inspiring music to our children as they fall asleep. The results have been amazing. What used to be a major struggle and battle zone has now turned into a very beautiful and pleasant experience most of the time.

After playing the music for several nights, the children now ask for music nearly every night to fall asleep to. It dispels fears. They are very seldom afraid of the dark because the music they listen to is filling their minds with beautiful thoughts and inspiring words.

Oh, that we could only let the beautiful powers of music fill our minds and souls. Music is important in our lives. Much more so than most of us have realized. Gladstone put it this way. "Music is one of the most forceful instruments for governing the mind and spirit of man," (*Ensign,* Jan. 1974, p. 28).

Hopefully, each of us will be more conscious of the magnificent power of music and also of some of its destructive powers so that we may enjoy it as one of God's greatest creations. Hopefully, music will become to us as it was to the poet Longfellow when he expressed, "Yet music is the prophet's art. Among one of the gifts that God has sent, one of the most magnificent," (Henry Wadsworth Longfellow, "Christus").

# Three

# "For My Soul Delighteth"

"The most inspired preaching is always
accompanied by beautiful, inspired music."

Harold B. Lee

"The life of 10-year-old Bobby Jenkins seemed to be filled with turmoil. His parents were divorced and his father remarried a fine woman, but she didn't seem to take the place of his real mother. To make matters worse, his oldest brother joined the army.

This left him at home with his 15-year-old brother, Tim. He was the one person Bobby could rely on. They had been through so much together. Even though Tim was five years older, they were as close as brothers could be.

Then one day Bobby received news which caused the bottom of his world to drop out. Tim had drowned in a senseless accident while swimming in the canal.

During the funeral, Bobby seemed to go numb. He had been hurt so many times, he didn't want to feel again.

Except for school and other necessary activities, he hibernated in his room. He turned on the radio to the hardest rock music he could find. Hour after hour, day after day, even while he slept, the music blared. With its loud and constant rhythm, he didn't have to think or feel. He could separate himself from the world which had hurt him so deeply.

After many weeks of this, his stepmother couldn't stand it any longer. In the middle of the night, while Bobby was sleeping, she tiptoed into his room and turned off the radio.

The next morning he poked his head into the kitchen and asked, 'Did you turn off my radio last night?'

Expecting the worst, his stepmother gently replied, 'Yes, I did.'

She didn't get the answer she had expected. Instead Bobby sat down at the table and softly shared the feelings of his heart.

'This morning when I woke up, Timmy appeared in my room. He told me he was happy and all was well. He said the Church is true and I should start reading the Book of Mormon. He told me lots of things which really made me happy.'

Bobby stopped just long enough to gain his composure, then continued. 'He said this was the fourth time he had received permission to visit me, but he couldn't come into my room because of the type of music I had on the radio.'

With a hint of emotion in his voice, this 10-year-old man, said, 'Thanks, Mom, for turning off my radio,''(Doug Bassett, *Kisses at the Window*, Hawkes Pub., pp. 75-76).

This true story written by Doug Bassett and shared with permission may seem a bit dramatic at first until you stop to consider the doctrine taught by the Prophet Joseph Smith and by Joseph F. Smith, sixth president of the church. Joseph Smith taught, "There are no angels who minister to this earth but those who do belong or have belonged to it."

Commenting on this statement President Joseph F. Smith said, "Hence, when messengers are sent to minister to the inhabitants of this earth, they are not strangers, but from the ranks of our kindred, friends. And fellow-beings and fellow-servants. . . . In like manner our fathers and mothers, brothers, sisters and friends who have passed away from this earth, having been faithful, and worthy to enjoy these rights and privileges, may have a mission given them to visit their relatives and friends upon the earth again, bringing from the divine Presence messages of love, of warning, or reproof and instruction, to those whom they had learned to love in the flesh," (Joseph F. Smith, *Gospel Doctrine*, pp. 435-436).

How often has the Lord tried to communicate with us, but we wouldn't let him because we had static in our receiving system? How often has our music or our videos been the source of that static? On the other hand, how often has the Lord communicated to us through music? Elder Bruce R. McKonkie made a profound statement concerning these questions when he said, "Music is part of the language of the Gods. It has been given to man so he can sing praises to the Lord. It is a means of expressing, with poetic words and in melodious tunes, the deep feelings of rejoicing and thanksgiving found in the hearts of those who have testimonies of the divine Sonship and who know of the wonders and glories wrought for them by the Father, Son, and Holy Spirit. Music is both in the voice and in the heart," (Bruce R. McConkie, *The Promised Messiah,* p. 553).

Is music important to the Lord? In chapter two we discussed Section 25:12 of the Doctrine & Covenants. We learned that the Lord delighted in the song of the heart and that the song of the righteous was a prayer unto him to be answered with blessings "upon their heads." Three books in the Old Testament are hymns written to be sung in the temple; Psalms, Proverbs and Songs of Solomon.

On the night Jesus was born we read that his birth was announced by angels singing. "And suddenly there was with the angel a multitude of the heavenly host praising God, and saying, "Glory to God in the highest, and on earth peace, good will toward men," (Luke 2:13-14).

One of the last things Jesus did on this earth before going into the Garden of Gethsemane to atone for our sins, the single greatest event in the history of the universe, was to sing a song with his friends. Mark 14:26 reads, "And when they had sung an hymn, they went out into the mount of Olives." Did Jesus understand the power of music to help prepare himself for the great ordeal that awaited him? And did he also understand the strength the apostles might need as they embarked on an uncharted journey? Perhaps this is why he sang with his friends and offered a "prayer unto God."

The last thing the Prophet Joseph Smith did on this earth before he was murdered by a mob, was listen to music. He had Brother John Taylor sing him "A Poor Wayfaring Man of Grief." Brother Taylor was singing while the mob broke into Carthage Jail and killed Joseph and his brother Hyrum. Music in praise of Christ and in thanksgiving was the last impression on the spirit of those two great heroes.

Is music important to the Lord? The Savior of the world and the prophet of the restoration both prepared for their last moments with music. Doctrine & Covenants 135:3 tells us, they have done more for the salvation of men in the world than any other two men who ever lived in it.

Many prophets of this dispensation have spoken explicitly of music as a missionary tool and as a tool to edify and uplift. President David O. McKay once remarked, "There can be no greater missionary work than to sing the songs of Zion among our friends who have not yet accepted this message of the restored gospel," (*Improvement Era,* Jan. 1959, p. 15).

President Heber J. Grant stated, "The singing of our sacred hymns written by the servants of God has a powerful effect in converting people to the principles of the gospel and in promoting peace and spiritual growth. Singing is a prayer unto the Lord," (*Improvement Era,* Sept. 1940, p 522).

President John Taylor wrote, "Music prevails in the heavens," (G. Homer Durham, *Gospel Kingdom,* Bookcraft, p. 62). If music prevails in the heavens are we, as mortals then, the authors of any song or are we simply translators of that which was already composed in more heavenly spheres? Is this divine origin of music the reason it has such a powerful effect upon the spirit of man and why the Lord can use it for so much good?

Once again music is a prayer unto the Lord. Along these lines President George Albert Smith told a moving story about the power of music to touch the hearts of men.

"Many years ago, two humble elders laboring in the Southern States Mission were walking through the woods and finally came out into a clearing where there was a humble cottage, the home of friends who were not members of the Church. Overlooking this clearing was a hill covered by large trees. It had been a warm day, and when the elders arrived, instead of going into the house, they took their chairs out on the shady porch to visit with the family.

"They didn't know that they were being watched or that danger threatened. They had come through a section of the country that was unfriendly, and having found a home where the family was friendly, they were grateful to the Lord for it.

"They were asked to sing, and they selected the hymn, 'Do What is Right,' and as they started to sing, there arrived on the brow of the hill above them a mob of armed horsemen. One of those men had previously threatened the missionaries and had kept watch for them on the road.

"These armed men had come there with the determination to drive those missionaries out, but as they arrived at the top of the hill, they heard these missionaries singing. The leader of the mob dismounted and looked down among the trees and saw the roof of the house, but he could not see the elders. They continued singing.

"One by one the men got off their horses. One by one they removed their hats, and when the last note had died away and the elders had finished their singing, the men remounted their horses and rode away, and the leader said to his companions, 'Men who sing like that are not the kind of men we have been told they are. These are good men.'

"The result was that the leader of the mob became converted to the church and later was baptized. I never hear that hymn sung, but I think of that very unusual experience when two missionaries, under the influence of the Spirit of God, turned the arms of the adversary away from them and brought repentance into the minds of those who had come to destroy them," (*Improvement Era*, March 1951, pp. 141-142).

Music is one of the ways that our Father can communicate to us. He can touch our hearts regardless of our language. There is no barrier. He may touch our emotions, our minds. He has always done so.

I think often of the incident related in I Samuel 16:14-23. An evil spirit had attacked Saul, the King of Israel. His servants suggested that they find someone who was a "cunning player of an harp" and play for Saul whenever the evil spirit was upon him. David, the son of Jesse the Bethlehemite, was the one chosen for the task. "And it came to pass when the evil spirit from God (which was not from God, JST) was upon Saul, that David took an harp and played it with his hand: so Saul was refreshed, and was well, and the evil spirit departed from him."

31

In considering the events in the life of Saul and how he rid himself of an evil spirit by listening to inspiring music, a question arises. If beautiful inspiring music can cause evil spirits to flee and depart, can uninspired, degrading, depressing music invite them in? Elder Boyd K. Packer answered this question. "Someone said recently that no music could be degrading, that music in and of itself is harmless and innocent. If that be true, then there should be some explanation for circumstances where local leaders have provided a building—expansive, light and inviting—and have assembled a party of young people dressed modestly, well-groomed with manners to match. Then over- magnified sounds of hard music are introduced and an influence pours into the room that is repellent to the spirit of God," (*Ensign,* Jan. 1974, p. 25).

Most of us have, at one time or another, felt a change in spirit because of the kind of music played in a location or circumstance. Music will generally do what it is written to do. If it is intended to agitate or depress, most of the time it will. Or if it is intended to mellow or pacify, it will. For this reason we would never prepare for a sacrament meeting by singing or playing heavy metal or punk rock. Yet on the other hand we would generally never prepare to participate in a football game by listening to the Mormon Tabernacle Choir.

Music is important to the Lord and he uses it for good and to accomplish many of his spiritual purposes. Elder Boyd K. Packer, again, has expressed how music has influenced him on occasion. He also gives some wise counsel to those gifted in this area. "I have been in places where I have felt insecure and unprepared. I have yearned inwardly in great agony for some power to pave the way or loosen my tongue, that an opportunity would not be lost because of my weakness and inadequacy. On more than a few occasions my prayers have been answered by the power of inspired music. I have been lifted above myself and beyond myself when the spirit of the Lord has poured in upon the meeting, drawn there by beautiful, appropriate music. I stand indebted to the gifted among us who have that unusual sense of spiritual propriety.

"Go to, then, you who are gifted, cultivate your gift. Develop it in any of the arts and in every worthy example of them. If you have the ability and the desire, seek a career or employ your talent as an avocation or cultivate it as a hobby. But in all ways bless others with it. Set a standard of excellence. Employ it in the secular sense to every worthy advantage but never use it profanely. Never express your gift unworthily. Increase our spiritual heritage in music, in art, in literature, in dance, in drama.

"When we have done it our activities will be a standard to the world. And our worship and devotion will remain as unique from the world as the Church is different from the world. Let the use of your gift be an expression of your devotion to him who has given it to you. We who do not share in it will set a high standard of expectation: 'for of him unto whom much is given much is required . . . ' D&C 82:3," ("The Arts and the Spirit of the Lord," Boyd K. Packer, BYU Twelve Stake Fireside, Provo, Utah, Feb. 1, 1976, p. 12).

Satan is well aware of this powerful medium and is trying desperately to distort it and use it to his advantage. Concerning this devious ploy, Elder Bruce R. McConkie wisely warned, "Unfortunately not all music is good and edifying. Lucifer uses much that goes by the name of music to lead people to that which does not edify and is not of God. Just as language can be used to bless or curse, so music is a means of singing praises to the Lord or of planting evil thoughts and desires in the minds of men," (Bruce R. McConkie, *The Promised Messiah*, Bookcraft, p. 553).

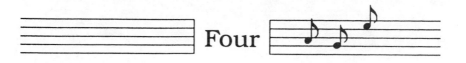

# Four

## Opposition In All Things

"Not every spirit, or vision, or singing, is of God.
The devil is an orator; he is powerful."

Joseph Smith, (*Teachings of the
Prophet Joseph Smith*, p. 162)

A few years ago I had the opportunity to teach seminary at Timpview High School in Provo, Utah. I was excited to begin a new year and looked forward with great anticipation to what the future held. I was somewhat apprehensive, however, about going to Timpview because it would be my first experience of teaching or attending school without spending my afternoons playing football or baseball or coaching. I knew I could do it, but I worried nevertheless.

I suppose that is why I enjoyed pep assemblies so much. It was an opportunity to feel many of the same feelings I had had as a player and as a coach. You have probably had the same experience—chills running down your arms and the back of your neck when you enter the gymnasium while the band is playing and the cheerleaders are cheering. It's exciting!

I remember one particular assembly before a big game. The cheerleaders had planned a special class competition involving cream pies. I don't remember all the details, but I do remember that some of the athletes, you know the type, the ones who all sit together and won't cheer except on rare occasions, got an idea to liven things up by throwing some of the pies at the cheerleaders. Somehow the activities the cheerleaders had planned were left in a barrage of pies being thrown, hairdos being ruined, and the student body cheering for the athletic culprits. I must admit, it was quite an experience.

Very little was said to these young men that I am aware of by the cheerleaders. Each girl allowed the boys to think they had really gained the upper hand and gotten away with a fast one. The pies were soon forgotten, and another pep assembly greeted us a few weeks later. This time, as we entered the gym, there were 12 caramel apples sitting on the floor at center court. Big, beautiful, brown caramel apples, waiting for someone to eat them.

When everyone was settled down and the band had ceased playing, the head cheerleader walked to the microphone and began to explain that morning's class competition. From a small piece of paper she read the names of six football players and challenged them to a candied apple-eating contest. As each name was read the responding young man came down to the basketball court with confidence, raising his hands as if in triumph, knowing that he could eat an apple faster than any girl.

Myself and another teacher were called upon to judge this historic event. The cheerleaders explained the rules to me, and I then explained them to the young men. The young men, however, were not overly concerned because each was proficient in eating and eating quickly. The only two rules were, (1) every apple on each team must be completely devoured, and (2) the girls were to be allowed a ten-second head start.

After hearing the rules, the young men decided on a game plan. They would not chew—just bite, swallow, bite, swallow, until each apple was gone. With such strategy the contest began.

The whistle blew, and the girls began to eat with great care and deliberate actions. The boys, on the other hand, stood watching, waiting for their winning opportunity.

When the second whistle blew, each young man, without any hesitation or forethought, lunged toward the caramel apple before him. With no table manners evident, they began to devour them with great haste—bite, swallow, bite, swallow. Then suddenly, in unison, as if a light switch had been turned on inside each boy, heads raised in shock and disbelief as they realized they were not eating candy-covered apples but candy-covered onions! The crowd roared when they realized what had happened. The cheerleaders, on the other hand, stood calmly, hands signaling the peace sign in recognition of their sly plan to deceive the football players.

By now these poor boys were looking as white as sheets and trying to get rid of the large bites of raw onion which were now floating throughout their systems. I'll never forget it! Those poor guys smelled like onions for quite some time, and it was not an easy task to rid themselves of the stench.

Since then I have told that story hundreds of times while speaking about music and its relationship to our actions, feelings, thoughts, and spirituality. In doing so I have thought very seriously about what happened that day at Timpview. The cheerleaders had made the onions appear so much like the apples that the football players could not tell the difference until the onions became a part of them and it was too late.

No one ever dreamed that those "sweet" young ladies would be so mischievous as to use something these young men loved so dearly—food—to get back at and deceive them.

When I ponder that story I always ask myself, "Would Satan try to do the same thing to deceive us?" Would he use the things we love the most to deceive us and bring us down to destruction? Could he even use music, which most of us love dearly, to deceive us?

In Doctrine and Covenants 50:2-3 the Lord told the Prophet Joseph Smith that one of Satan's major objectives is to deceive us: "Behold, verily I say unto you, that there are many spirits which are false spirits, which have gone forth in the earth, deceiving the world. And also Satan hath sought to deceive you, that he might overthrow you." He is the champion of all liars and does not care one bit about you or me. His only desire is to seek our misery.

Of course he would use music! Without question he knows that music is one of God's greatest tools for good ever created. He must be aware that it is one of the most important and powerful influences in our lives. So, if he has this knowledge, would he not use music as one of his greatest counterfeits of all time? After, all, isn't listening to music one of the first things we do each morning, and one of the last things we do before we go to bed at night?

Of course Satan would use music to his advantage if he could. II Nephi 2:11 states: "For it must needs be, that there is an opposition in all things." To me that means that whenever God creates something that is good, true, and beautiful, Satan, in his devious way, comes up with something that is false, counterfeit, and ugly, yet appears to be similar to our Father's creation. He acts, if you will, in much the same manner that the cheerleaders did with the onions. He tries to deceive us into partaking of that music or music videos which are false, counterfeit, and ugly in hopes that we will not detect it until it is a part of us or too late altogether.

If there were no opposition we would have no freedom of choice. Without freedom to choose we would have a very difficult time existing. In fact, as the prophet Lehi taught, there would be no purpose in the end of our creation. There would be no righteousness because there would be no wickedness. And if there were no righteousness he says there would be no happiness, (see 2 Nephi 2:13). We must have opposites. We must have choice.

How do many of us feel when we are made or forced to do something? Many of us rebel because we do not like to be told every single thing that we should do. When a parent yells down the hall, commanding the teenager to "turn that garbage down," it's very easy for the teenager to turn the volume up rather than down. It is not necessarily right, but so often it is the case. Without the freedom of choice we lose our valuable gift of agency.

The essence of agency was taught to me by a great teacher when he said, "To tell is to preach. To ask is to teach." Perhaps this is why the Savior said, "Come follow me," not forcing or pushing, but asking and then leading the way.

Of course with this agency we must also realize that there is deep and heavy responsibilty. The Lord instructed us in Section 58 of the Doctrine and Covenants that we are agents unto ourselves. We are free to choose. But if we have to be told and commanded in all things "we are slothful and unwise servants, wherefore we receive no reward." Nephi instructed us in a very similar manner in 2 Nephi 2:27. "Wherefore, men are free according to the flesh; and all things are given them which are expedient unto man. And they are free to choose liberty and eternal life, through the great Mediator of all men, or to choose captivity and death, according to the captivity and power of the devil; for he seeketh that all men might be miserable like unto himself." It seems obvious that the Lord has allowed us to choose for ourselves but has not taken away the responsibility for the choice.

Elder Bernard P. Brockbank of the First Quorum of the Seventy has said: "Young people, do you think Satan has music in his program? Do you think the Lord has music in his program? Satan's music has a way of destroying the godliness within a human soul, and there is some of the hard rock music that is definitely not from the Lord. It will tear down your spiritual strength and your divine nature. Don't get involved in it. When you feel that rhythm of hard rock becoming part and fiber of your soul, get away from it while you are young enough. Just remember, Satan will try to lure you away with convincing and deceitful practices so that you hardly know you are walking down the road with him," (Bernard P. Brockbank, Glasgow Area Conference, June 21, 1972).

Thomas Edison has said, "Music is the only sensual gratification in which mankind may indulge to excess without injury to their moral or religious feeling," (*Ensign*, Jan. 1974, p. 25). Perhaps that was true in his day, but is it in ours? Some of today's music appears to have moved away from such innocence. Remember we must never fear the truth.

Obtaining and recognizing the Spirit is perhaps the most essential asset in determining that music which will have a beneficial effect upon us. In the fourth chapter of Jacob verse 13 we learn that "the Spirit speaketh the truth and lieth not. Wherefore, it speaketh of things as they really are, and of things as they really will be." If we have the spirit we will see things as they really are and not just as they appear on the outside. I know of no greater guide that could be given to anyone for detecting Satan's ways. We cannot forget, that "that which doth not edify is not of God, and is darkness," (D&C 50:23).

Many, many years ago before any of us came to earth, an incident took place that may help us understand why Satan would take musical apples and counterfeit them into musical onions to be used for destructive purposes. This event is commonly referred to as the War in Heaven.

"And there was war in heaven: Michael and his angels fought against the dragon; and the dragon fought and his angels,"

"And the great dragon was cast out, that old serpent, called the Devil, and Satan, which deceiveth the whole world: he was cast out into the earth, and his angels were cast out with him."

"Therefore rejoice, ye heavens, and ye that dwell in them. Woe to the inhabiters of the earth and of the sea! for the devil is come down unto you, having great wrath, because he knoweth that he hath but a short time."

"And the dragon was wroth with the woman, (the Church of Jesus Christ) and went to make war with the remnant of her seed, which keep the commandments of God, and have the testimony of Jesus Christ," (Revelation 12:7, 9,12,17).

From studying these passages of scripture, it seems obvious that Satan is trying to concentrate his attack on those who are striving to do good and who have testimonies of Jesus Christ. He wants to destroy those who are going to have an effect for good in this life. He wants to destroy the strong before they become an opposition to him here as they were in the war in heaven.

"Lucifer desires all good people. He even tempted the Savior on at least three recorded occasions. . . . Satan wants all men, but especially is he anxious for the leading men who have influence. Perhaps he might try much harder to claim men who are likely to be his greatest opposition, men in high places who could persuade many others not to become servants to Satan. It seems that missionaries are special targets. Satan takes a special interest in all such workers," (Spencer W. Kimball, *The Miracle of Forgiveness*, p. 175).

Satan still remembers the premortal existence and is aware of those individuals that fought most valiantly against him and he "walketh about, seeking whom he may devour," (I Peter 5:8). He drew a third of the host of heaven with him (see Revelation 12:4) and when they were cast out, that third of the host of heaven came to earth and brought with them the knowledge they had previously possessed. Our knowledge, on the other hand, was temporarily taken from us through our birth into mortality.

Perhaps this is why at the time of the birth of the great prophet

Moses, the adversary put it into the heart of Pharaoh to have all the baby boys drowned in the River Nile. He obviously knew that if he did not kill Moses the baby, he would have to deal with Moses the prophet.

In the meridian of time, when Jesus was born into the world, Satan put it into the heart of Herod to have all of the young children under the age of two, within his jurisdiction, killed in hopes of destroying Jesus the baby so that he did not have to deal with Jesus, the Messiah, the Redeemer, the Son of God.

Later, in the spring of 1820 when Joseph Smith was but 14 years of age, he went into a grove of trees and a power of darkness rested upon him. It continued until Joseph felt like it would crush the very life out of his body; but through his prayer, finally a pillar of light descended and he was released from the power of Satan. Satan knew that he would have to reckon with Joseph, the prophet of the restoration, (LeGrand Richards, *Ensign,* May 1981, p. 31-33).

Were many of today's youth with Moses, the Savior, and the Prophet Joseph Smith as part of the "noble and great ones" spoken of by Abraham? (See Abraham 3:22). Is this why Satan is trying so desperately to destroy them? Will they become, "leading men and women of influence?" Perhaps this is why it seems that "all hell has broken loose" and why it is so difficult to carry on in "doing good continually."

This is one of the major reasons I shiver when I hear young people or their parents say, "Oh come on now, it doesn't really matter what I listen to, does it? I mean, after all, I'm more mature for my age and I can handle it." How often have you heard, "It doesn't affect me the way it does other people?" How often have those famous last words, "I can handle it," been spoken just before disaster or sorrow disassembled a once happy, flowering life?

If the adversary can convince us that it makes little difference what we listen to, watch, or take into our systems, then we have become his. It does make a difference. I marvel that young people or parents would ever consider fighting Satan on his territory. It terrifies me. Can they honestly feel they have a chance to survive?

George Albert Smith said, "My grandfather used to say to his family, 'There is a line of demarkation, well defined, between the

41

Lord's territory and the devil's. If you will stay on the Lord's side of the line, you will be under his influence and will have no desire to do wrong; but if you cross to the devil's side of the line one inch, you are in the tempter's power, and if he is successful, you will not be able to think or even reason properly, because you will have lost the Spirit of the Lord,' " (Spencer W. Kimball, *The Miracle of Forgiveness,* p. 232).

It is hoped that all parents will show as much interest in the records, tapes, and videos their children purchase as they would the reading material they bring into the home. Most parents would not allow their children to purchase pornographic magazines or videos, yet sometimes unknowingly provide money for music that can be every bit as damaging in its influence.

Who do we think we are when we feel we can do battle with a being such as Lucifer and win, especially on his territory? Can we, day after day, continue to walk through a spiritual mire of inappropriate entertainment and remain unscathed or unmarred? If we choose to make unwise decisions in our entertainment, it cannot help but have a direct relationship to our actions, feelings, thoughts, and spirituality.

May the reader who feels that it makes little difference what type of music is listened to, regardless of the content, be reminded that Doctrine & Covenants 76:25-26 tells us, that Satan was so powerful in the pre-existence that he "was in authority in the presence of God." And that when he was cast out of God's presence "the heavens wept over him."

He has spent thousands of years learning the weaknesses of men. We as mortals are nearsighted when we believe that after a few short years on earth, with no knowledge of what went before, that we are a match for the likes of him.

I am not saying that if we listen to or watch certain kinds of music that have negative connotations that we will become involved in the negative behaviors being suggested. For instance, we may not necessarily become involved in drugs, parental hatred, witchcraft, devil worship or the occult. I am saying, however, we may stop doing the most important things.

As has been expressed so often by church leaders, we cannot

hold hands with Satan and God at the same time. We have to let go of one or the other. When we worship certain types of music or any other worldly idol more than spiritual things, we are holding hands with Satan and are walking in darkness. The chances are greater for us to become insensitive to the things that are spiritual; to lose interest and motivation to attend church or to go on a mission. Doubts and fears will cloud our minds. We will begin to walk in our own way, after the image of our own god, "whose image is in the likeness of the world, and whose substance is that of an idol," (D&C 1:16). If we lose our desire to be missionaries, to read scriptures, to pray, to marry in the temple as suggested, have we not then been drastically or even fatally affected by the music? We must cling to the iron rod and follow the prophets of God.

Things are not the same as in years past. The differences between the world and the Church, when it comes to music and most other areas appears wider in our day than ever before. It is a "good versus evil" scenerio being acted out before us. Satan is employing his forces against all that is good. But as President David O. McKay has said, "We can through obedience to the commandments of God stand as lights whose rays will penetrate a sin stained world," (*Improvement Era*, June 1968, p. 5).

As each of us fights this constant battle with the evil one concerning music or videos or movies and every other facet of our lives, may we keep in mind and treasure the words of Elders Robert L. Backman, Vaughn J. Featherstone and Rex D. Pinegar. This message was given to all young men in the church. I believe it can apply to young women as well. "Oh, our beloved young men of the church, we live in a great and evil day. Never have the powers of darkness, evil, and perversion covered the earth as they do in this generation. This is the season in the Lord's affairs that the greatest generation of young men in the history of the world is being called forth. Our work is at hand. It is not a time to indulge or live an undisciplined life. It is a time to rally to the banner of our Master, to declare with unwavering allegience our loyalty to his great cause. It is a time to be noble and pure, to live lives disciplined like no other generation. It is a season for a 'Spartan' life, a committed life, a conquering life.

"This generation of young men is going to do deeds never done before. You are going to accomplish the seemingly impossible because you are on His errand. Your generation will fight the greatest army of Satanic hosts ever assembled. You will be severely outnumbered. You will need a deep and abiding faith in Christ to survive—and you will survive. The Lord and his servants will triumph, we do know that,"(*Church News,* May 9, 1981, p. 9).

If, as suggested, by these three general authorities, the only way to overcome the spiritual holocaust taking place in our world today, is to establish a deep and abiding faith in Christ, the question must be asked, is your entertainment leading you to Christ or away from Him? We must ponder deeply this question and be honest with ourselves. With music being such a powerful medium for good or evil, we had better learn how to make the right and appropriate decisions. We must learn to choose between the musical apples and the musical onions.

# Five

## Making the Music Decision

"Of every tree of the garden thou mayest freely eat,
"But of the tree of the knowledge of good and evil,
thou shall not eat of it, nevertheless, thou mayest
choose for thyself, for it is given unto thee,"

Moses 3:16-17.

In the College of Education at Brigham Young University, there was a message on a bulletin board that has had a profound effect on my teaching philosophy as well as my personal life. It depicts a man fishing and another man being given a fish. The inscription reads: "Give a man a fish and he has food for a day. Teach that man to fish and he has food for the rest of his life."

I have pondered deeply over that saying as a teacher, father, and priesthood leader. I don't know if I have learned a more valuable lesson. In fact, it reminds me of a story about a fleet of fishing boats that docked each afternoon for years at the same pier. Each day as they entered the dock, the ship hands would clean their fish and throw the remains into the water. The sea gulls in the area would flock each evening to the pier hoping to find dinner and take part of it back to their young.

For years the sea gulls obtained plenty of food. They never had to work for themselves. The fishermen provided everything. As a result the sea gulls never learned to fish.

Then one day the fishermen and their ships did not return to the familiar pier but went in search of more fertile waters. As a result, the sea gulls missed their evening meal. Days passed and no ships, thus, no fish. Each passing day brought death to large numbers of birds. Eventually, most of the sea gulls in the region died. They had been hand fed for so long they had not learned one of the most basic and simple elements of life—to feed themselves!

Have we have become like the birds at the pier? Do we want so much for someone else to tell us what we should and shouldn't do that we do not learn the most basic and simple procedures for making our own decisions and choices?

It is likely that many may criticize this approach and may feel that it is very important to have all of the details, and a specific list of groups, stars and bands to avoid. However, each person can learn to choose for himself, without a current pop music chart, if they will not be afraid of the truth and learn to apply correct principles. So often when we get caught up in the specifics it is very easy to cause the very thing we try to prevent because we talk about it too much and in too much detail. We incite and inspire ideas that were previously, perhaps, not even thought of by the listener. We invoke or titillate curiosity.

As was previously mentioned, one of the major problems in music seems to be choosing between the "apples" and the "onions." There is much that is good and beautiful. There is also much that is false, counterfeit, and ugly, yet appears to be good.

How does a person choose? Perhaps one of the greatest blessings we enjoy in this life is that our Father in Heaven has not left us alone to make these difficult decisions.

The scriptures and the teachings of church leaders are filled with ways of helping us to evaluate the music and then choose for ourselves. We must learn to follow the direction of the Lord or we, like the young football players at Timpview, may partake of the "onions" and not even be aware of it.

Satan has done such a masterful job in counterfeiting his music, that without some assistance, it is not an easy task to distinguish the "apples" from the "onions." For this reason it is important to use eternal principles rather than the specifics of the day to make our choices. The artists may change but these principles never change. "What I the Lord have spoken, I have spoken, and I excuse not myself; and though the heavens and the earth pass away, my word shall not pass away, but shall all be fulfilled, whether by mine own voice or by the voice of my servants, it is the same," (D&C 1:38).

In Moroni 7:12-19 is perhaps one of the most explicit ways

that the Lord has provided for us to discern Satan and his counterfeits. This passage teaches us that we may know the difference between good and evil music just as assuredly as we know the difference between night and day.

"Wherefore, all things which are good cometh of God; and that which is evil cometh of the devil; for the devil is an enemy unto God, and fighteth against him continually, and inviteth and enticeth to sin, and to do that which is evil continually.

"But behold, that which is of God inviteth and enticeth to do good continually; wherefore, every thing which inviteth and enticeth to do good, and to love God, and to serve him, is inspired of God.

"Wherefore, take heed, my beloved brethren, that ye do not judge that which is evil to be of God, or that which is good and of God to be of the devil.

"For behold, my brethren, it is given unto you to judge, that ye may know good from evil; and the way to judge is as plain, that ye may know with a perfect knowledge, as the daylight is from the dark night.

"For behold, the Spirit of Christ is given to every man, that he may know good from evil; wherefore, I show unto you the way to judge; for every thing which inviteth to do good, and to persuade to believe in Christ, is sent forth by the power and gift of Christ; wherefore ye may know with a perfect knowledge it is of God.

"But whatsoever thing persuadeth men to do evil, and believe not in Christ, and deny him, and serve not God, then ye may know with a perfect knowledge it is of the devil; for after this manner doth the devil work, for he persuadeth no man to do good, no, not one; neither do his angels; neither do they who subject themselves unto him," (Moroni 7:12-17).

Again, never fearing truth becomes the key. The prophet Mormon, as he wrote these words to his son Moroni, obviously had a specific purpose for telling us in verse 16 that this is "the way" and not simply "a way" of choosing between good and evil. It also seems clear that verse 17 is not necessarily saying that all music must be of a religious nature in order to be good or appropriate.

There is much of today's music that we may well enjoy if we avoid certain types.

President Ezra Taft Benson stated, "We encourage you to listen to uplifting music, both popular and classical, that builds the spirit," (*Ensign,* Nov. 1986, p. 84). Again, I need not go down a list of groups that are good and bad. Verse 17 has the answer. If our music persuades us to do evil and believe not in Christ and deny him and serve not God, in any way, regardless of how much we enjoy it, or how popular it is or who performs it, we know with a perfect knowledge it is not of God but is of the devil and has one major purpose and that is our destruction.

President Gordon B. Hinckley has taught us, "Some would have us believe that the area between good and evil is largely gray and that it is difficult to determine what is right and what is wrong. For any who so believe, I recommend this beautiful statement by Moroni found in the Book of Mormon." He then quotes Moroni 7:16. Continuing on he said, "Let us establish in our lives the habits of reading those things which will strengthen our faith in the Lord Jesus Christ, the Savior of the world. He is the pivotal figure of our theology and our faith," (*Ensign,* May 1983, p. 80).

Let us likewise establish in our lives the habit of listening to that music or watching those videos that will strengthen our faith in the Lord Jesus Christ. Making this decision is sometimes difficult. It is also important to realize that if we take away that which is inappropriate, we must replace it with something good or we'll go right back to that which we abandoned. In an age where there are so many voices, which one will we choose to follow? As Sister Elaine Cannon has so beautifully put it, "Since there are so many voices around us it seems vital that we hear his," ("How Do I Choose," May 1980). However if we're going to make these appropriate decisions we must be somewhat educated in the process.

In considering the counsel given in Moroni chapter 7 there are some very important things to remember. Larry Bastian, former chairman of the Church Youth Music Committee, has commented, "There are at least three important persons who participate in each musical experience. First is the composer, who writes the melody and suggests a harmonic and rhythmic treatment. That which he seeks to communicate is then interpreted by an arranger or performer, who may treat the music in such a fashion as to communicate exactly the opposite from that intended by the composer.

"The third important person is the listener. Our musical tastes are the result of conditioning and personal experience. Every person responds to music, then, in his own unique fashion.

"The key to discerning the quality of music lies in what it communicates to us individually and personally. Perhaps, we Latter-Day Saints have not often enough asked ourselves the question: 'What does this music say to me?' Considering the influence of evil in the affairs of today's world, especially in contemporary entertainment, we should ask it often.

"If one can answer that a song is spiritually inspiring or that it urges him to see himself in a more noble perspective, then that music is good. If the music just entertains or momentarily lifts the spirits, then it has a useful place. If it makes him want to respond in a carnal, sensual way or to consider unrighteous desires, then that music should be avoided.

"Sometimes the environment in which music is heard has an effect of its own. For example, a song that sounds pleasant and refreshing on the stereo at home may make a different impression in a remote corner of a darkened room with the music at a blaring level.

"Music is the language of the heart and of the spirit. It often communicates on a level where words are inadequate. It is on this level that it must be evaluated. We may not understand sometimes why we respond as we do, but we should measure the response, choose that which is compatible with our understanding of the eternal nature of things, and reject the rest," (*Ensign*, July 1974, p. 14).

Another important standard to use while making a decision on music is the 13th Article of Faith.

"We believe in being honest, true, chaste, benevolent, virtuous, and in doing good to all men; indeed, we may say that we follow the admonition of Paul—We believe all things, we hope all things, we have endured many things, and hope to be able to endure all things. If there is anything virtuous, lovely, or of good report or praiseworthy, we seek after these things."

Is our music virtuous, lovely, of good report or praiseworthy? If it is, wonderful! It is good, and we'll never go wrong by listening to it. On the other hand, if it is not, then we know with a perfect knowledge, as the daylight is from the dark night, that it is not of God and should not be part of our lives. Does it persuade us to be honest, true, chaste, benevolvent, virtuous and to do good to all men. If so, again, wonderful. If not, we certainly know where it comes from.

A third important way of choosing is found in the Doctrine & Covenants 50:23- 25 which reads, "And that which doth not edify is not of God, and is darkness."

"That which is of God is light; and he that receiveth light, and continueth in God, receiveth more light; and that light groweth brighter and brighter until the perfect day.

"And again, verily I say unto you, and I say it that you may know the truth, that you may chase darkness from among you."

Perhaps chasing this darkness from among us is one of life's greatest challenges. However, if we will but apply these correct and eternal principles taught in this chapter we will better understand why we make the choices we make and what Omni 1:25 means when it says, "For there is nothing which is good save it comes from the Lord: and that which is evil cometh from the devil."

President Kimball counseled, "The arts should build. We cannot give in to the ways of the world with regard to the realm of art. . . . Brigham Young said there is 'no music in hell.' Our art must be the kind which edifies man, which takes into account his immortal nature, and which prepares us for heaven, not hell," (Edward L. Kimball, *Teachings of Spencer W. Kimball,* p. 394).

"Our youth," Elder Boyd K. Packer has said, "have been brought up on a diet of music that is loud and fast, more intended to agitate than to pacify, more intended to excite than to calm. Even so, there is a breadth of it, some soft enough to be innocent and appealing to our youth, and that which is hard, and that is where the problem is . . . the music of the drug and the hard rock culture. Such music has little virtue and it is repellent to the spirit of God . . . There is much of today's music that they may well enjoy, if they avoid the hard kind," (*Ensign*, Jan. 1974, pp. 25, 27).

Now that we have some appropriate and surefire ways of choosing, let's put our new found knowledge to use by asking ourselves four specific questions.

**1. Lyrics.** What if the music is beautiful, lovely, and serene, but the words or lyrics are inappropriate or contrary to the teachings of Christ? Can the song be good, and should we listen to it? Nearly always when I speak on this subject parents will say, "Well, I can't understand a single word they say. How do they listen to that garbage?" The younger people generally respond with, "I don't listen to the words. I just like the rhythm and the beat."

It has been discovered that it makes little difference, to most, if you understand the words or if you pay attention to them or not. For many, the minute words are put together with music it's cemented into the memory. It's amazing how we often sing or hum tunes with words that we would never dream of speaking. It's also amazing how my students have a difficult time memorizing one scripture, but they know every word of every song in the Top 40. I love the simple phrase, "A song will outlive all sermons in the memory."

While thumbing through a local sales brochure one day I noticed that it gave some interesting figures. "Children remember 10% heard, 40% story, 60% visual aids, and 90% that is taught by music. Teach your children through music." If these figures are accurate, it is obvious that words accompanied by music play a far greater role in our lives than most of us have ever before realized.

Some time ago I was driving down the freeway with my radio playing when a song by the Beatles came on. In an instant my mind rushed back to the late 60s, and I began to daydream while singing and pondering. I caught hold of some pleasant memories from my past and remembered some activities I had participated in while listening to that song so many years before. Of course, as I sang, I never even missed a comma. I remembered every single word. It had been at least ten to twelve years since I had heard that song but the lyrics were vivid in my memory.

Joseph F. Smith taught, "May I say to you that in reality a man cannot forget anything? He may have a lapse of memory; he may not be able to recall at the moment a thing that he knows, or words that he has spoken; he may not have the power at his will to call up these events and words; but let God Almighty touch the mainspring of the memory, and awaken recollection, and you will find then that you have not even forgotten a single idle word that you have spoken? I believe the word of God to be true and, therefore, I warn the youth of Zion, as well as those who are advanced in years, to beware of saying wicked things, of speaking evil, and taking in vain the name of sacred things and sacred beings. Guard your words, that you may not offend even man, much less offend God," (*Improvement Era,* May 1903, pp. 503-504).

It's easy to say that the words are not important or that they're not the major part of the song. However, when they are constantly in our minds it's hard to throw out the scriptural teaching, As a man "thinketh in his heart, so is he," (Proverbs 23:7). Becoming what we think about most of the time is not a new concept to the advertising industry. Very few commercials on television or radio are not accompanied by catchy jingles or memorable musical scores.

*The Wall Street Journal* printed an interesting article concerning advertisers using musical groups to reach young consumers. The findings were remarkable. For years advertisers wanted nothing to do with the flamboyance of the rock industry. However, it didn't take very long for them to change their minds when dollars were involved. Most rock stars are much more business oriented now than in times past and money is the name of the game. For this purpose many advertisers have used rock 'n' roll particularly to sell their products. Often times they bring back old songs from the 60s and 70s as jingles put to words concerning the product in order to have some type of recognition with the consumer, (see *The Wall Street Journal,* July 28, 1983).

With the advent of music videos, lyrics now become extremely important in the selling of products. If Saturday morning advertisers can sell a box of cereal in 30 seconds, can music promoters sell us a lifestyle in a three minute video?

With MTV and other video stations the shape of fashion has changed in the United States. It has made extreme clothing totally acceptable. Outrageous clothing that would have taken possibly 15 years to get visibility now is popular within a week because of its use in videos. (See *TV Week*, *Deseret News*, March, 10, 1985, p. 17).

Simply put, the lyrics do make a difference and are programmed into our minds whether we like it or not. Very few of us purposefully memorize the words to daily commercials. But with repetition, they often times become a part of us, programmed into our thought patterns by their connection with unforgettable tunes.

Phrases or words are often learned easier when accompanied by music. They are easily remembered because they are put together in a rhythmic fashion that makes them easy to recall. Certain types of rote learning can be enhanced with some types of music. For example, by putting the names of the books of the *Old* and *New Testament* or the *Book of Mormon* to specific tunes, the memorizing of the books in order is much simpler and in many cases very much easier to recall. Perhaps this is why President John Taylor remarked, "If I had time to enter into this subject alone I could show you upon scientific principles that man himself is a self-registering machine, his eyes, his ears, his nose, the touch, the tastes, and all various senses of the body, are so many media whereby man lays up for himself a record," (John Taylor, *Journal of Discourses*, 26:31).

**2. Music.** The next major question when choosing music or other forms of entertainment has to be the music itself. What if the words are magnificent, inspiring, and lovely, but the music itself affects you in a negative way, or in a way that is contrary to the teachings of Christ? Should we be listening to it? Once more I realize that these are specific questions and sometimes they may be considered fanatical, but we must understand that there is a real war being fought here and every avenue must be explored and looked at.

Can music, in and of itself regardless of lyrical content, have an influence on the way we act, think, and feel? My reserach has shown that music will do to a person, generally, what it is written to do. It can excite. It can mellow. It can relax. It can agitate. It can lift spiritually. It can depress, and have many other profound influences upon us.

Music has always played a major role in my preparation for speaking, for spiritual communication, for athletic competitions, and in many areas of my life. On most occasions it has accomplished the desired result. I must admit that I never did listen to the Taberncale Choir before a big game because it would do exactly what it was meant to do—get me in a spiritual frame of mind. Don't get me wrong, I always wanted to be spiritual but playing in a major college football game was not the time to ask the linebacker across the line the "Golden Questions." Maybe after the game but not during it. I would have been killed! However, I should quickly add that I never listened to "psyche" music appropriate for before games to prepare for a testimony meeting. Different types of music do cause different types of reactions and feelings. Therefore, if the music is "persuading us to do evil, or believe not in Christ or deny him, or serve not God", then we know it is inappropriate and should not be listened to.

Hopefully, we have established the fact that music alone, without lyrical content, can have a profound influence on us. To illustrate this point I wish to refer once again to television and the movies. Even before movies had sound there was always an organ or a piano to create mood and to communicate feeling or mood to the viewer. What would a movie be like without music? How would we ever know during a scary film that someone was hiding in the closet? How would you know when to be romantic, when to be nervous, when to be excited, when to cheer? If music were eliminated from movies I'm afraid moviegoers would seek out new forms of entertainment. Obvoiusly it would simply be too boring to maintain our attention.

My favorite example of music having a significant effect during a movie is the the classic motion picture "Jaws." During the opening scene, if there had been no music, the movie would have lost its impact because the person viewing the picture would have no idea what was going on. However, with the music, the entire storyline is made clear.

The movie begins with a young girl swimming near the beach. As she swims, she suddenly goes into jerking motions and has a look of terror on her face. Without music, the viewer wouldn't know if this young woman has stubbed her toe on the pier or hit her feet on the jagged coral below. By adding the music to the scene, the viewer begins biting fingernails, wincing with fear, curling up in their seat, vocally screaming, "Get out! Get out!" Even without seeing anything the audience knows the great white shark is about to attack that girl. With the music, when the girl's body goes into jerking motions, the crowd moans with terror and vows never again to go swimming in the ocean.

Again, music will do what it is written to do. We, therefore, must be careful and judge wisely.

The producer, the performer, the arranger all have certain objectives that they wish to achieve whether it be to stimulate, depress, agitate, inspire, or uplift. However, we must remember that the name of the game in the music industry or any media industry, for that matter, is to make money. It is a business and that which is going to increase revenues, good or bad, is that which is going to be sold and produced not only in America but everywhere. Money is the name of the game. It has always been thus. Money will determine what music is produced. Money talks.

In the pursuit of material wealth and fame, many have lost their way. They have been blinded by the subtle craftiness of men who lie in wait to deceive. Their greed glands get stuck. They begin to serve another god other than our Father in Heaven and sometimes innocently, they don't even realize what is taking place. Thus, there is a large amount in the media that is not edifying nor uplifing but that is degrading and leading us in a negative direction. It is often easy to take a low standard of morality because it sells.

This idea of lowering standards in order to achieve wealth and money is not new. It has been going on since the beginning of time. The Savior taught the Nephites in III Nephi 27:32 that "they will sell me for silver and for gold, and for that which moth doth corrupt and which thieves can break through and steal."

Cain sold himself for his brother's flocks, (see Moses 5:8-33). Judas Iscariot sold himself and our Master for 30 pieces of silver, (see Matthew 26:14-16). The ancient Israelites were no different. They were worshipping false gods and selling themselves to do evil, (see 2 Kings 17:16-17).

The Nephites also fell prey to this plague of seeking after that which is of no lasting importance and became involved with Satan and his counterfeits. After nearly two hundred years of perfect peace and harmony they became proud and thus fell into Satan's trap, (see Mormon 1:19; 2:10).

Knowing what went on in ancient times, is it any wonder then that the same types of activities and secret societies continue in our day? Why are we so alarmed when we read in the daily newspaper about all of the secret combinations that are being brought to light? The adversary and his followers are still trying to destroy all that is good, (see D&C 76:29). Music is simply one of their methods.

Are there connections between the occult and certain types of music? Are witchcraft and devil worship thriving in our society today? The answer is clear, yes. Some performers are brought into the realms of the occult for various reasons, for money, for power, or for the desire to succeed, and these musicians will do anything that it takes to get to the top. They actually "sell themselves to do evil in the sight of the Lord" in hopes of achieving success, praise and increase.

By delving into matters of devil worship or the occult in detail we sometimes cause the very thing we are trying to prevent. It is unnecessary to get involved in a detailed discussion concerning these matters. The scriptures are replete with information concerning the effects of secret societies.

Perhaps the wisest counsel of all on this entire matter came from the ancient prophet Alma as he turned over the sacred records to his son Helaman. "And now, my son, I command you that ye retain all their oaths, and their covenants, and their agreements in their secret abominations; yea, and all their signs and their wonders ye shall keep from this people, that they know them not, lest peradventure they should fall into darkness also and be destroyed," (Alma 37:27).

Now we return to the original second question. If the words are good but the music is bad should we be involved in it? Or if there are known negative subliminal messages or if the music persuades us to act, think, or feel contrary to the teachings of Christ, should we be involved in such types of music? No. However, I admonish each reader to seek for that which is virtuous, lovely, of good report and praiseworthy in contemporary as well as classical music.

**3. Album or Tape Covers.** Should we listen to that music contained on the record, tape or compact disc if the covers are promoting immorality, drug abuse, violence and destruction, or covered with gross illustrations, signs of witchcraft, devil worhsip or the occult? At first this may seem easy, but I don't feel the answer is that simple. I often hear young people argue, "But Brother Christianson, I don't listen to the covers." I understand that and realize that the covers may have nothing to do with the music inside, and it may just be a technique to promote sales. However, if the artist or composer is willing to do anything to sell it, that tells us something. Again I refer to Moroni 7 and the 13th article of faith. If the covers are contrary to the teachings of Christ it's difficult to see that the music inside them could be appropriate. I refuse to give specific details of the signs of devil worship and witchcraft. I do not want to be responsible for causing people to get involved with this type of activity. But if there are things on the album covers that are blatantly out of touch with the teachings of Christ, I think we need to understand that there could be problems on the inside.

One day while walking through a local record store I had an experience that I have not been able to forget. I was interested in finding a particular album that many of my students had purchased. While scanning the selections, my eyes caught a glimpse of another popular album. The title of the record was "Mob Rules."

There were some figures dressed in robes with hoods over their heads with no faces. Between them was a piece of canvas streaked with red paint. As I observed the album more closely, I realized that the streaks of red paint were not just streaks but a picture of Satan. As I recognized the face, which was the central figure of the picture, I realized why the figures had no faces. When a mob rules, individuality flees. I was then sickened by the thought that it was a mob that took Jesus and crucified him at Golgotha. It was a mob that murdered the Prophet Joseph Smith. It was an uncontrolled mob that caused the Mountain Meadow Massacre. I quickly put the album down and left the store without finding the album I was originally looking for. I was truly sickened to think that some of my students felt that "Mob Rules" was just a catchy title and nothing more. I am not picking on this particular group, but if the covers are not in accordance with the standards we try so diligently to live, we know they do not measure up to our guideline in Moroni 7.

How would we feel if we had to give the prophet a ride in our car and had an inappropriate tape on the dashboard or in the glove compartment and he saw it? Would we be embarrassed and want to hide some of the tapes in our collection. I think that's a good indication as to whether our music, the album covers or whatever are appropriate.

**4. Music Videos.** To introduce this powerful music medium, I wish to share a brief story. Many years ago, as a missionary, I had an experience in the dry desert of New Mexico that affected me forever. My companion and I had the assignment to pick up several new missionaries from the airport and drive them to their various assignments. After a short meeting, we took the new elders to our favorite eating establishment and then proceeded with the task before us. As we drove around the city that evening, I began to feel tired and nauseated. I shrugged it off as nothing serious.

That night, however, the ill feelings increased. As I tried to sleep, my stomach turned and my head was spinning. Beads of sweat soaked my body, then moments later I felt like I was sitting at the North Pole. Chills wracked my body. The illness seemed relentless. After several miserable trips to the bathroom and hours of hot flashes and chills, I resolved that life was no longer worth living. If God were going to take my life, this was the perfect place. With these overly dramatic thoughts, I pleaded with the heavens to release me from the bondage of my illness and let me leave this mortal existence.

Fortunately for me, my prayers weren't answered. The next day after a priesthood blessing and some scientific investigation, I not only recovered but discovered that I had suffered from severe food poisoning. I don't recall a time in my life when I felt more sick. That spoiled food was devastating.

As I ponder the memories of that dreaded night, I wonder why so many people feel they can continue a diet of "spoiled" spiritual food and never suffer spiritual ailments. I believe we are as much what we listen to and watch as we are what we eat. Just as the spoiled food made me want to die, so can a diet of smut affect our desire for spiritual existence. President Kimball stated: "Teach your children to avoid smut as the plague it is. As citizens, join in the fight against obscenity in your communities. Do not be lulled into inaction by the pornographic profiteers who say that to remove obscenity is to deny people the rights of free choice. Do not let them masquerade licentiousness as liberty. Precious souls are at stake—souls that are near and dear to each of us," (Edward L. Kimball, *Teachings of the Spencer W. Kimball*, p. 285). When each of us considers the precious souls at stake, our menu of listening and viewing material must be considered closely.

With the advent of music videos in the music marketplace, as well as the introduction of television programs such as Music Television (MTV), the 24- hour cable music station, and Friday Night Videos, other serious questions arise. What if the video of a song promotes or portrays attitudes, behaviors, and feelings contrary to the teachings of Christ or his prophets? Should we participate in viewing them and will they truly affect our actions, feeling, thoughts, and spirituality? Does seeing rock 'n' roll, or other types of music, on TV or on videos, where it is packaged for concise easy assimilation, make it more vital or add a missing depth to the song's expression? Again, if a 30-second commercial can sell a box of cereal, can a three-minute video sell a lifestyle?

Turn on MTV any time when young people are present, and you can be assured that most other activities will cease and soon the program will have a mesmerized audience drinking deeply from its pictures.

There is something about seeing the music that is captivating. Today's listeners spend countless hours viewing what past generations only listened to. With the visual images being broadcast simultaneously with the audio, the purpose and position of the composer and performer is brought home with force and fervor. Nothing, as in times past, is left to the imagination of the listener. The purpose and intent of the song is acted out before their eyes in vivid details and unforgettable fashion. After going through the video once or twice, the images are planted firmly in our minds and can be recalled quickly and in detail with the slightest stimulus.

This medium is really nothing new to the marketplace. News reporters have used the visual technique to powerize their stories since the inception of the movie theater and television.

I vividly remember going to the movie house in my home town and watching a newsreel before every major movie. Everything from war to horse racing was broadcast because few people, in those days, had the luxury of in-home televisions. Believe it or not, I still remember some of those flittering black and white newscasts.

Dan Rather, anchorman for the CBS Evening News, makes a great case for why newspaper readers should also watch TV newscasts. "If you read a good newspaper every day you're going to know most, if not all, of what's on the evening news and probably a lot more But you won't have seen it. I think there's a difference between reading about the war and seeing some of it," (*TV Show Biz Magazine*, Jan. 15-21, 1984, p. 41).

"Social workers are almost unanimous in sighting the influence of the popular media, television, rock music, videos and movies in propelling the trend toward pernicious sexuality. One survey has shown that in the course of a year the average viewer sees more than 9,000 scenes of suggested sexual intercourse or innuendo on prime time TV," (*Time Magazine*, Dec. 9, 1985, p.81).

The thing that scares me is that with such a barrage of sexuality the message being broadcast is that to be sophisticated we have to be sexually hip. We have to know what's really going on. One author states that we don't even buy toothpaste to clean our teeth anymore, but we buy it to be sexually attractive or to make sure we have fresh smelling breath when we have an encounter with someone of the opposite sex.

Many people in the music, record, tape, and video business without question, have picked up on one of the "hottest" ways of selling known to man. Letting people see and feel the product. Unfortunately, many of the selling techniques center around pornography, violence, and occult activities. Why? Because it sells to the masses! We must not forget that the major purpose for music videos and music TV programs is not primarily to educate but to sell. Money is the name of the game even if spiritual ill health results.

Pornography has taken a swing to videos, rather than the printed page, because people can actually see and fantasize more graphically and in more detail than they could on the printed page. In the 80s many pornographic magazines have been fighting for survival but porn videos are booming.

One of the best-selling groups of the entire decade of the 80's is quoted as saying, "We're the American youth and youth is about sex, drugs, pizza and more sex. We're intellectuals on a crotch level. We're the guys in high school your parents warned you to stay away from. That's what we're like on stage and off. The kids won't buy albums from phonies." One of the members of the band then goes on to say, "I know people who pray for us every day. They can't save us. We're gone," (*Rockin' in the 80s*, pp. 94-95).

Can this barrage of sexually explicit material and violence fail to have a profound effect upon the rising generations?

Victor B. Cline, a clinical psychologist, professor at the University of Utah, and a nationally regarded expert on the influence of pornography on society, wrote a stirring article entitled, "Obscenity—How It Affects Us. How We Can Deal With It." In this article the problem of seeing what we are listening to is brought masterfully into focus. He states: "The outside world truly has entered into our homes—into the family room, the kitchen, and the bedroom. The seriousness of the problem has prompted this examination of a sensitive and distasteful subject.

"The media have a great potential to teach, inspire, inform and entertain, but they may also corrupt, degrade, and pervert. They have the power to influence profoundly for good or evil all aspects of our values and feelings, as well as our behavior. We are affected by what we choose to expose ourselves to.

"For example, I have a letter from a 14-year-old girl telling of the death of her 10-year-old brother by hanging. With naive innocence, he had imitated the scene of a mock hanging he had witnessed in an evening television movie. He thought he could escape death as the actor in the movie had. He didn't.

"As a clinical psychologist, I see examples almost daily of gracious and good people (all ages, both sexes) of exemplary upbringing who have become addicted to viewing violence. Many have also cultivated an appetite for voyeuristically viewing stimulating, sexually explicit scenes of mulitple adulteries, rape, or the seduction of innocents—all in living color and accompanied by a memorable musical score.

"Evil is presented as attractive and good. Destructive behaviors are marketed as exciting and rewarding. Often humor is used to make pornography, rape, or the loss of innocence entertaining and palatable.

"But what starts out as a spectator sport introduces into one's brain a vast library of antisocial fantasies. These have the potential, much research suggests, of eventually being acted out—to the destruction of the individual and others around him.

"I have found that four things typically happen to some people who become immersed in erotic or pornographic material.

"First, they become addicted. They get hooked on it and come back for more and more.

"Second, their desire for it escalates. They soon need rougher and more explicit material to get the same kicks and excitement.

"Third, they become desensitized to the abnormality of the behavior portrayed. In time, they accept and embrace what at first had shocked and offended them.

"Fourth, eventually there is a tendency and temptation to act out what they have witnessed. Appetite has been whetted and conscience anesthetized . . .

"Those who witness this porno-violence in commercial cinema, on cable television, or on a rented videocassette—and who allow their children to view it—in my judgment do great injury to themselves and their children. This exposure creates false images and feelings about men and women and sexuality and raises the possibility that the viewer may be conditioned into practicing sexual deviancy. For, as much evidence has suggested, all sexual deviations are learned, not inherited," (*Ensign*, April 1984, pp. 33-34).

No wonder many people are losing interest in spiritual matters. They feed themselves, spiritually, on a diet that is totally nonnutritious. They become as sick spiritually as I had become physically from my spoiled dinner. In fact, President Kimball has stated that the poisoning that takes place from viewing unwholesome material is worse than partaking of poisonous food. He said:

"Each person must keep himself clean and free from lusts. He must shun ugly, polluted thoughts and acts as he would an enemy. Pornography and erotic stories and pictures are worse than polluted food. Shun them," (Edward L. Kimball, *Teachings of Spencer W. Kimball*, p. 283).

The classic words of Charles Dickens ring in our ears. "It was the worst of times. It was the best of times." We live during a time period when more is available for our good and comfort than at any other time in the earth's history. However, as far as sin and corruption are concerned, we live in some of the worst of times. Yet if we can remember the moving words of Joshua when our peers and others seek to have us choose music or any other thing that is contrary to godliness, we will always have the "best of times."

Joshua beseeched, "Choose you this day whom ye will serve; . . . but as for me and my house, we will serve the Lord," (Joshua 24:15).

Good luck in your fishing!

# Six

# Music And Our Actions, Feelings, And Thoughts

Recently my wife and I attended a concert performed by the Mormon Youth Symphony and Choir. It was a marvelous production. The music was uplifting, edifying, and resounding. It left me with a wonderful feeling. However, I almost missed the feeling because of those sitting near me.

Just to my right was a young man sitting with his mother, totally engrossed in the production. At times he would have to restrain himself from clapping. At other times he was tapping his feet. Then without any notice or warning, tears would roll down his cheeks as the orchestra would play songs that touched his heart and feelings. I found myself watching him entranced by the effect the music had upon him. Then my eyes caught an older gentleman sitting two rows in front of me. He was singing the words to himself and conducting the music as if he were in front of the stand. He was moving his hands in a 4/4 beat and then a 2/4 beat matching the beat or rhythm of the song being performed.

I could not help but ask myself the question, And people say music doesn't have any effect upon the way we act, think, or feel? I was not only entertained and educated by the symphony and choir but by the audience.

One of the most fascinating of phenomena in the world is the manner in which music affects human thought, feeling, and action—the ingredients of the individual's whole spiritual being. I never cease being amazed, as I travel, how hairstyles, dress, speech, attitude, social behavior, recreational choices, and other activities are affected, each in its own way, by the music an individual devotes himself to, and by the heroes and heroines of that particular type of music.

Open your own eyes. See for yourself. As you go to the store or to a ballgame, note how many of the styles you see had their beginning on a poster or album cover, in a popular movie, in a music fad promoted by radio, video, or music television. Indeed, much of our modern environment is affected by music.

In his talk entitled "Satan's Thrust—Youth," President Ezra Taft Benson quoted the late Richard Nibley, former professor of music at Snow College, Ephraim, Utah: "Music creates atmosphere. Atmosphere creates environment. Environment influences behavior," (*Ensign*, Dec. 1971, p. 53). Dr. Nibley goes on to explain that the mechanics of the atmosphere-environment-behavior relationship are rhythm or beat, volume, repetition, gyration, darkness, and flashing light.

Many consider rhythm to be the very heart of music, because of its profound effect on the individual. It is natural to tap the foot, the fingers, or a pencil as we listen to music. Small children are interesting to watch, because of their total honesty and lack of inhibition. Without having been taught the intricacies of music, they instinctively begin to move in time with whatever music they happen to hear. It is rhythm or beat that causes such actions.

Dr. Nibley explains this further: "Rhythm is the most physical element in music. It is the only element in music that can exist in bodily movement without benefit of sound. A mind dulled by drugs or alcohol can still respond to beat," (*Ensign*, Dec. 1971, p. 53).

"With the ears completely blocked, the body still responds to sound. This is because we "hear" not only with our ears, but also with our bodies," (John Diamond, *Your Body Doesn't Lie*, Warner Books, 1979, p. 155).

This potential for hypnosis is in harmony with the comments of two famous singers who quit the business when they realized what their music was doing to people. One asserted that the music he performed "clouds the senses and hypnotizes the brain. When you get people at their weakest point you can preach into the sub-conscious what we want to say," (*The Plain Truth*, Sept. 1980, p. 14).

That idea is a little frightening. On this point, Dr. Reid Nibley, professor of music at Brigham Young University, has written, "Sustained chords lower blood pressure; crisp, repeated chords raise it. Loud volume stimulates responses of hormone secretion in addition to nervous and muscular tension," (*BYU Today*, April 1980, p. 15).

A fascinating study has been conducted by Dr. John Diamond and is recorded in his book, *Your Body Doesn't Lie* (New York, Warner Books, 1979.) Dr. Diamond is a behavioral kinesiologist and has made an indepth study of the function of the body and one of the major influences on the body, he has found, is music. His discoveries are quite remarkable but very logical. His major thesis concerning music is that because of the heartbeat and the rhythm of the music, our bodies are profoundly affected. The da da dah, da da dah beat known in poetry as the anapestic beat is very common in many rock records. However, it appears to have a different effect when used with music than when used in poetry. "The rock beat appears to be addictive; repeated exposure to it causes one to seek it. It becomes the beat of choice," (*Your Body Doesn't Lie*, p. 165). He goes on and discusses that our bodies are physically affected and that our muscles are weakened by this particular beat. On the other hand, many muscles are strengthened with other types of beats and rhythms. It is almost impossible for the muscle to have full strength while listening to the anapestic beat.

He does mention that not all rock numbers have this weakening effect nor does any particular group necessarily have the effect consistently. He mentions that the earlier songs of rock 'n' roll did not have the effect that the hard rock music of today does. He tested over 20,000 records of all types of music and found that the only other passage, other than hard rock, that caused the muscles to go weak was a short segment of Haitian voodoo drumming.

In classical music he found only two instances that produced musical weakness. One is at the conclusion of Stravinsky's *Rites of Spring* and the other at the conclusion of Ravel's *La Valse*. In both instances, the composer was attempting to convey chaos which he obviously did quite successfully, (see *Your Body Doesn't Lie*, p.160-3).

This particular rock beat is not only, as was mentioned before, addictive and repeated exposure does cause one to seek it, but it throws the entire body into a state of alarm. It causes major changes to occur in children. Their performance in school decreases and hyperactivity and restlessness increase, (*Your Body Doesn't Lie*, p. 164).

In adults, Dr. Diamond found a decreased work output, increased errors, general inefficiency, reduced decision-making capacity on the job, and a nagging feeling that things just aren't right. He goes on to say that the major problem he sees is a loss of energy for no apparent reason. He also found that the academic records of many school children improved considerably after they stopped listening to rock music while studying.

Now once again, I'm not on a crusade against any type of music, but it seems obvious that if certain types of music, particularly hard rock, have this type of an effect, we should be wise and not be digesting that material that could negatively affect us.

A number of studies have been conducted at universities across the country concerning the effects of music on the physical aspects of the human being. For example the behavior of unruly and hyperactive children is markedly improved by playing background music. Popular children's records being played result in marked improvement in children's behavior. Also by such procedures productivity of hyperactive children in a school room setting is enhanced, (*Family Weekly*, Feb. 22, 1976, p. 11).

It has also been found that unborn children within the womb are profoundly affected by the music their mother listens to or is exposed to. Children who are read to or talked to or have good music stimulation while in the womb have been found to react to sound and vocal structure better than those who have not received such stimulation. They are also found to be soothed much more easily when music is played, (*USA Weekend*, Nov. 8-10, 1985, p. 31).

Music has such a profound effect on us that even while driving in stressful traffic it has been found to reduce accidents when you have your car radio on. I know this sounds crazy, but institutional studies have shown that music played at peak accident periods has resulted in a lower accident rate because the music can do a great deal to offset the effect of nerve-sapping tensions and aggressive driver reactions, which often build up during these stressful time periods. Some music, (mood, instrumental, choir and semi-classical) have even increased the production of mothers' milk while nursing by as much as 50% to 150%, (*Family Weekly*, Oct. 4, 1970, p. 14) Does music have an effect on our bodies and our actions? Of course it does. And we would be very foolish to think otherwise. Therefore we must, as mentioned so many times in this text, listen to only that which is going to have a positive effect upon us.

What about our thoughts and feelings? Are they as profoundly affected by the music we listen to as are our actions? The evidence again overwhelmingly is yes.

In chapter two we discussed what a profound effect music has in our everyday lives. Most of us go about our lives having no real thought of how the music we listen to or the videos we see, or the words we sing, affect our minds and our feelings. We had better be careful what we let filter through our minds, "For our words will condemn us, yea, all our works will condemn us; we shall not be found spotless; and our thoughts will also condemn us" (Alma 12:14). We are, or will become, what we think about most of the time. Again, we are as much what we listen to and watch as we are what we eat. It becomes as much a part of our lives as the onions became a part of my student.

Napoleon Hill, in his classic book *Think and Grow Rich* said, "Our brains become magnetized with the dominating thoughts which we hold in our minds. And by means with which no man is familiar, these magnets attract to us the forces, the people, the circumstances of life which harmonize with the nature of our dominating thoughts," (p. 28). The lyrics, the words, the scenes from the videos, constantly flowing through our minds cannot help but have a profound effect on what we think and how we feel.

As was also discussed earlier, we can in reality forget nothing. Every experience, every word becomes a part of our lives and of our organism. In recent years this fact has been demonstrated by world authorities during brain surgery. Doctors Penfield and Roberts of the Montreal Neurological Institute have literally confirmed that we don't forget anything. It is all stored in our brains. It is just a simple matter of recall, not of remembering or forgetting but of bringing it back. During brain surgery when they stimulated certain brain cells with an electrode, the patients on whom they were working reported the sensation of reliving scenes from their past. Their recall was so vivid that all details were present including sounds, colors and odors. Not just remembering but reliving the experiences, (Denis Waitley, *The Psychology of Winning*, Berkley Books, 1984, p. 95).

Where does music fit in in all of this? Music is, as I have already mentioned, one of the greatest ways that we have to learn things. In studies conducted at New York University the playing of certain types of music was found to inspire many persons to score better on various mental tests than they did without the influence of music. Then at Louisiana State University investigators compared the performance of students on mental tests while classical music was being played, when jazz was listened to, when rock 'n' roll was played, and also with no music. Students made the lowest scores on the tests when rock 'n' roll was played, (*Family Weekly*, Oct. 4, 1970 p. 14). Again, I'm not attacking rock 'n' roll, I'm simply pointing out the finding of the researchers.

As far as music affecting our thought processes, how many of us learned the ABCs or the books of the *Old* and the *New Testament* with music? There is a reason. It is easier to remember when accompanied by a good little catchy tune. Again, the advertisers are capitalizing on this fact by giving us many of their messages with short brisk tunes that we never forget.

When it comes to learning and music and retaining information, Dr. Georgie Losinov, a leading psychiatrist from Sophia, Bulgaria, has done a tremendous amount of work, and the results of much of his work are recorded in a book entitled, *Super Learning*. Dr. Losinov developed a method of cue-reinforced learning which is sometimes known as suggestology or suggestopedic learning. He uses music and rhythmic or repeated listening using the music as a relaxation technique to help people or students learn at a very rapid rate things such as foreign languages and lists of factual data. The results of his research are stunning to educators because of the ability a person has to learn when using the powerful force of music along with other scientific methods, (*Super Learning*, Dell Publishing, New York, 1979, p. 62-76).

When people become depressed, psychological studies show that people resist strenuous verbal efforts to cheer them up. But when using music, because it affects people on a feeling rather than a thinking level, investigators at a leading university found that depressed subjects respond favorably to lively exciting music, (*Family Weekly*, Oct. 4, 1970, p. 14).

For example, when a young person becomes angry in the home, what does he or she do? It has been my experience that not all by any means, but many young people retreat to their rooms and crank up the music as loud as possible. Why? Because the music "harmonizes" with the feelings they feel. We usually want to listen to music that agrees with how we want to feel about ourselves and others. Using music that is selected to coincide with the actual moods of a person is known by psychologists as the iso-principle. Using the iso- principle, the music matching the mood, we learn that if a person is depressed, downbeat music is matched to the depressed mood. Then by stages the music is changed to a happy mood, thereby altering the mood of the subject. As one investigator pointed out, matching the mood of the music to the mood of the person is necessary because otherwise the subject will reject the music. But by degrees we can shift the music and carry the subject's mood into a more tranquil state, (*Family Weekly*, Feb. 22, 1976, p. 11).

Knowing this little bit of information, does it answer some questions to why so many people today are angry with society, with the world, with themselves? Take a look at the music they listen to. What videos are they watching? Are they filled with violence, anger? Have we found violence as the cure to all of societies woes?

As a football player in college, I remember how excited I would get during the pre-game warmups. At the south end zone, huge speakers boomed out the tunes of the hometown radio station. Without question such music helped get me ready to play the game. Many times when I went snow or waterskiing, the music of my stereo hyped me into a carefree, even reckless state of mind.

President Spencer W. Kimball commented on the close relationship between the instruments played and the feelings they induce: "Musical sounds can be put together in such a way that they can express feelings—from the most profoundly exalted to the most abjectly vulgar. Or rather, these musical sounds induce in the listener feelings which he responds to, and the response he makes to these sounds has been called a 'gesture of the spirit.' Thus, music can act upon our senses to produce or induce feelings of reverence, humility, fervor, assurance, or other feelings attuned to the spirit of worship. When music is performed in church which conveys 'a gesture' other than that which is associated with worship, . . . the musical 'gesture' departs from or conflicts with the appropriate representation of feelings of worship," (Edward L. Kimball, *Teachings of Spencer W. Kimball*, p. 519).

As far as thoughts are concerned, I think we all struggle at one time or another. In today's world it is very difficult to blot from our perceptions all the vulgar and profane the world puts before us. If, however, we provide a place for our thoughts to go, we can control them. They need not control us. The old adage applies: "You can't keep birds from flying over your head, but you can keep them from making a nest in your hair." We may not always be able to control what flits into our minds, but we can control how long it stays there.

Without virtuous thoughts, it is easy to find ourselves lacking in confidence, in having the Holy Ghost as our constant companion, and in understanding the doctrine of the priesthood, (see D&C 121:45-46).

I especially like what Elder Boyd K. Packer has said about music and our thoughts: "Probably the greatest challenge to people of any age, particularly young people, and the most difficult thing you will face in mortal life is to learn to control your thoughts. As a man 'thinketh in his heart, so is he.' (Proverbs 23:7). One who can control his thoughts has conquered himself.

"I want to tell you young people about one way you can learn to control your thoughts, and it has to do with music.

"The mind is like a stage. Except when we are asleep the curtain is always up. There is always some act being performed on that stage. It may be a comedy, a tragedy, interesting or dull, good or bad; but always there is some act playing on the stage of the mind.

"If you can control your thoughts, you can overcome habits, even degrading personal habits. If you can learn to master them you will have a happy life.

"This is what I would teach you. Choose from among the sacred music of the church a favorite hymn, one with words that are uplifting and music that is reverent, one that makes you feel something akin to inspiration. Remember President Lee's counsel; perhaps 'I Am A Child of God' would do. Go over it in your mind carefully. Memorize it. Even though you have had no musical training, you can think through a hymn.

"Now, use this hymn as the place for your thoughts to go. Make it your emergency channel. Whenever you find these shady actors have slipped from the sidelines of your thinking onto the stage of your mind, put on this record, as it were.

"As the music begins and as the words form in your thoughts, the unworthy ones will slip shamefully away. It will change the whole mood on the stage of your mind. Because it is uplifting and clean, the baser thoughts will disappear. For while virtue, by choice, will not associate with filth, evil cannot tolerate the presence of light. In due time you will find yourself, on occasion, humming the music inwardly," (*Ensign*, Jan. 1974, pp. 27-8).

This formula certainly works for me. My hymn is "I Know That My Redeemer Lives." I sing it when evil thoughts try to enter my mind. My mind has, in fact, become much like a stereo system that goes to automatic, as the record begins to play the evil thought departs.

Elder Packer goes on, "Once you learn to clear the stage of your mind from unworthy thoughts, keep it busy with learning worthwhile things. Change your environment so that you have things about you that will inspire good and uplifting thoughts. Keep busy with things that are righteous.

"Young people, you cannot afford to fill your mind with the unworthy hard music of our day. It is not harmless. It can welcome onto the stage of your mind unworthy thoughts and set the tempo to which they dance and to which you may act.

"You degrade yourself when you identify with all of those things which seem now to surround such extremes in music: the shabbiness, the irreverence, the immorality, and the addictions. Such music as that is not worthy of you. You should have self-respect.

"You are a son or a daughter of Almighty God. He has inspired a world full of wonderful things to learn and do, uplifting music of many kinds that you may enjoy," (*Ensign*, Jan. 1974, pp. 27-8).

Human beings are not the only creations of God that are drastically affected by various types of music. Plants and various animals are also. Moses 3:5 tells us, "For I, the Lord God, created all things, of which I have spoken, spiritually, before they were naturally upon the face of the earth." If all things were created spiritually, which they were, then the old adage, "Music hath charms to soothe the savage beast," may well apply in the animal and plant kingdom.

The reader may enjoy and be interested in a few experiments concerning plants and animals and how they responded to various types of music. These experiments may sound a little crazy. But if all things were created spiritually before they were created temporally it seems logical that they would respond differently to that which is of God and that which is not.

The first involves a Tulsa, Oklahoma, radio station that dedicates soft, mellow songs to the cows each morning because they are so touchy around milking time. The music soothes these animals and they produce better milk. It is also found that acid rock, some experts say, almost dries the cows up, (*Family Weekly*, Jan. 27, 1985, p. 18).

The second experiement deals with a young girl from Ogden, Utah, who decided to run an experiment using her sagebrush lizard and her Northeastern fence lizard. The lizards were exposed to various types of music for ten days. She entered her experiment in the 1981 Weber Regional Science Fair and her findings were later reported in the *Ogden Standard Examiner*.

"For the first few days she played classical music—mostly symphonies, but some instrumental arrangements of hymns. The lizards responded ecstatically to the serious music.

"They climbed up on the rocks to get closer to the speakers. They lifted their faces up to the source of the music.

" The report indicated that they also grew during their classical concerts. Each of them gained about a gram.

"The next series of music the lizards were subjected to was country western. They lost their uplift and paced back and forth across the terrarium, acting as if they were ornery with each other. They also lost a half a gram in weight.

"The final series of music was hard rock. During this concert they lost another half a gram apiece and buried themselves in the sand, even to the point of hiding their heads," (*Ogden Standard Examiner*, 1981).

There is, at this time, no way of judging the validity of this girl's findings, but her results are very interesting.

Dr. Reid Nibley reported to the BYU student body a third set of experiments. His source was an article in the *Denver Post* (June 21, 1970), "What Acid Rock Did to the Petunias Shouldn't Happen to Our Teenagers."

"A series of experiments conducted for nearly two years by Mrs. Dorothy Retallack of Denver showed that assorted plants have been killed by exposing them to rock music.

"She discovered that just three hours of acid rock a day shrivels young squash plants and flattens philodendrons and crumbles corn in less than a month.

"Mrs. Retallack piped to her plants—placed in controlled environment chambers—music from two Denver radio stations. One group of plants was exposed to a rock station and another group to a semi-classical station.

"The results: 'The petunias listening to rock refused to bloom. Those on classical developed six beautiful blooms. By the end of the second week, the 'rock' petunias were leaning away from the radio and showing very erratic growth. The 'classical' petunias were all leaning toward the sound. Within a month all plants exposed to rock music died,' " (*BYU Today*, April 1980, p. 15).

Mrs. Retallack conducted further experiments on various groups and types of vegetable plants with similar results.

These experiments are cited only as points of interest—and they are interesting. On reading of such experiments, I wonder just how much influence some of our popular music today is having not only on inidvidual lives but on our entire environment.

Because of my interest in this aspect of music, I find it immensely enjoyable to expose those to whom I speak to a variety of music. (Of course, I am careful in the pieces I select—as you should be too, if you decide to try an experiment of your own). In spite of the good times I and the audiences often have, there are always a few people who, for some reason, are reluctant to admit the effects of music on them until they are actually challenged in a learning-by-doing situation.

I like to start by tuning up and down the FM radio dial. The reactions of young and old alike are hilarious as they hear the songs they either adore or despise.

A good station to start with is an "elevator music" type station. It is also the kind of music you would hear in the dentist's office or the supermarket. Many parents smile when they hear it, but most of the younger generation plead with me to turn it off. When I ask them what the station is, most of them know the correct answer. "How come you know it if you never listen to it?" I ask them? Invariably someone responds, "It reminds me of my mother!" A classic admission that music does affect our feelings.

Next I move to some country western music. People start clapping and hee- hawing, preparing to mount an imaginary horse and ride off into the sunset.

As I go through various selections of music, I watch forehead movement and facial expression. I hear whispered conversations stimulated by what is heard. It is indeed quite a show.

Inevitably when I play a current popular tune, or one that was popular 10 to 30 years ago, I see a young girl or older woman begin to blush. You know the rest. She nudges a neighbor or her husband with her elbow and says, "Why, that's our song." Music stimulates memories, and listeners have to share them.

Sometimes I have played the themes from the various Rocky movies. Unless you yourself see this experiment or try it yourself, it's hard to believe what happens. People take deep breaths and bulge their chests out as if they could conquer the world. Heads begin to jerk with the beat, hands are raised above the head in clenched fists, and some people start punching their neighbors like a punching bag. I don't have to tell people what the titles are; they respond to feelings that stir inside them.

Sometimes I have a difficult time controlling myself. I picture in my mind's eye a drill team at a football game during half-time, and I even feel an impulse to act accordingly. My arms fly out in front of me, my head moves from side to side, and my legs want to march. I doubt if I would ever behave like that without the aid of that tune.

After the audience sees how much their thoughts, feelings, and actions are influenced by the music they hear, I change the entire mood of the meeting by playing songs by the Tabernacle Choir, or a soft, peaceful piece with a background of rolling waves and faintly screaming seagulls. There is a metamorphosis in the audience. Suddenly a vibrant, excited group becomes calm, sleepy, and docile.

People are eager to express what they feel and think in that peaceful minute. I enjoy their responses because they are basically all the same. They recite the scenes that were implanted in their minds by the music. After the spirit of the meeting has been set by the peaceful music, we are ready to discuss the effects of music on our spirits.

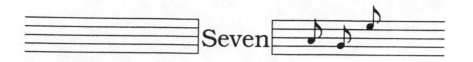

# Listening To A Prophet's Voice

"The Lord expects more from you than from any previous generation. This is because you are charged with preparing the way for the second coming of the Lord Jesus Christ."

(Victor L. Brown)

**M**any years ago I taught a couple of classes that were particularly difficult to handle. Some students would trail into class with little interest in learning anything and especially about the Savior or the scriptures that taught about him. I was troubled. Often I would go home discouraged, wanting to leave the teaching profession. It seemed as if very few students were being affected. It felt like I was wasting my time. Then one day after class a student brought me a popular album and asked me to listen to the words of a song contained on it.

We went into my office and played the song, listening closely to the music as well as the lyrics. The music was depressing. It made me feel like I was being chased by some creature of the unknown through a graveyard at night in the fog. It was so depressing that I wanted to take it off. But the student insisted on me hearing the words. He felt I would be interested in their message. I have never been able to forget what I heard that afternoon.

"Well I don't want no preacher telling me about a God in the sky.

No I don't want no one telling me where I'm gonna go when I die.

I'm gonna live my life don't want people telling me what to do.

I'll just believe in myself cause no one else is true." (Black Sabbath,"Under the Sun," Vol. 4, Warner Bro. Records Inc.)

These words, coupled with music that would go well in a horror movie, were not the worst lyrics I had heard but were preaching some of the greatest false doctrine ever taught, namely, that a person need not worry about God nor what happens after death and that an individual is just that, an individual with no need for others. He must live his own life, depending on no one. Could this be one of the reasons so many seemed so disinterested?

If a person, young or old, has a constant diet of such music, how is he or she likely to respond when parents, teachers, or friends, admonish: "Gather round, today I would like to teach you about God in the sky. Today, I would really like to discuss where you go when you die."

Not all people would respond the same way. But knowing what we know about music, if a person never listened to much else, what would his reactions likely be? Would spiritual matters lose their importance? Would statements such as, "You cant' tell me what to do," or "It's my life, and if I want to throw it away it's none of your business," or "Just leave me alone!" become the norm?

When considering such questions and this experience with my student years ago, my heart aches. Is it really their life? Does a person have the right to "mess" it up or live it any way they choose? Though we may have the free agency to choose for ourselves, it is vital to remember that we are responsible and accountable for our choices, (see Revelation 20:12-13). As the old saying goes, you can't pick up one end of the stick without picking up the other.

Nearly 2,000 years ago, the greatest blood that ever coursed through veins was spilt on the ground of a dusty garden and on a cross so that you and I could be forgiven of our sins and live forever. To put it simply, the greatest sacrifice in the history of this universe, and the highest price ever paid for anything, were given for you and me. Through the atoning sacrifice of Jesus Christ we were each bought for a price. The price being the life of the Son of God.

Yes, we were bought. The price paid was so high that most of us have but a faint notion as to its significance. The apostle Paul taught us well on this subject. "What? know ye not that your body is the temple of the Holy Ghost which is in you, which ye have of God, and ye are not your own?

"For ye are bought with a price: therefore glorify God in your body, and in your spirit, which are God's," (I Corinthians 6:19-20).

When considering this ulitmate act of love, my heartstrings are wrenched with pain, yet my eyes cry tears of joy. My soul sings out the words, "Oh, it is wonderful that he should care for me, enough to die for me," (Hymns, p. 193).

To those who still contend that, "It's my life, and I'll listen to or do anything I please and it's none of your business," perhaps a little insight into what happened that memorable night in Gethsemane and the following day in Jerusalem will be helpful in understanding why our lives are not our own.

Christ himself gave the prophet Joseph Smith a brief glimpse as to what transpired that night. "For behold, I, God, have suffered these things for all, that they might not suffer if they would repent;

"But if they would not repent they must suffer even as I;

" Which suffering caused myself, even God, the greatest of all, to tremble because of pain, and to bleed at every pore, and to suffer both body and spirit—and would that I might not drink the bitter cup, and shrink—

"Nevertheless, glory be to the Father, and I partook and finished my preparations unto the children of men," (D&C 19:16-19).

In the gospel of Luke we also learn that His suffering was so intense that an angel was sent to strengthen him: "Father, if thou be willing, remove this cup from me: nevertheless not my will, but thine, be done.

"And there appeared an angel unto him from heaven, strengthening him.

"And being in an agony he prayed more earnestly: and his sweat was as it were great drops of blood falling down to the ground," (Luke 22:42-44).

Can any of us understand such love and devotion? "The thought makes reason stare."

This agony in the garden was not the end of his suffering. After this experience our Lord was taken like a criminal and stripped naked. He was beaten, spit upon, mocked, scourged, slapped across the face, and crucified on a cross between two thieves. All this He did without offering any resistance. And at the end, He plead with his Father and our Father to "forgive them; for they know not what they do," (Luke 23:34).

Why did He pay such a price? Why do we oftentimes, along with the world, reject His ultimate sacrifice? Perhaps, the words of the prophet Nephi answer these two questions best. "And the world, because of their iniquity, shall judge him to be a thing of naught; wherefore they scourge him, and he suffereth it; and they smite him, and he suffereth it. Yea, they spit upon him, and he suffereth it, because of his loving kindness and his long-suffering towards the children of men," (I Nephi 19:9).

Let us not think of this price as a "thing of naught." Let us not "trample under our feet the Holy One of Israel."

Now let us refer back to the words of the song at the beginning of this chapter. After contemplating such a heavy topic as the atonement of Christ, can you see why Satan would, in his various methods, try to get people to believe that it is unimportant to learn about "God in the sky" or "Where are you going when you die?" To me, it appears obvious that if he can deceive us into believing false doctrine it can have a catastrophic effect on our spirituality.

Heber J. Grant said, "The more beautiful the music by which false doctrine is sung, the more dangerous it becomes," (G. Homer Durham, *Gospel Standards*, p. 170).

This is where I find the thickest walls of resistance as I speak on this subject. Many understand that much of the music they listen to is not so good, but they honestly believe that it will not affect their spirituality.

"They're just kids, for heavens sake, let them have their fun. They'll grow out of it," is a fairly common statement heard from some parents and leaders. Or some have commented, "Our kids would never do that. Besides some of the music isn't that bad, is it?" Some even contend that, "If we don't allow them to listen to it they'll just go somewhere else to get it."

I cringe when I hear songs promoting immorality, drug abuse, or rebellion being played at church functions simply because that is the only way we can get some of our youth to come to the activities.

President J. Reuben Clark commented concerning such philosophies. "We may not, under our duty, provide or tolerate an unwholesome amusement on the theory that if we do not provide it the youth will go elsewhere to get it. We could hardly set up a roulette table in the church amusement hall for gambling purposes, with the excuse that if we do not provide it the youth will go to a gambling hall to gamble. We can never really hold our youth thus. Our task is to help the home plant better standards in the minds of the youth," (*Ensign*, Jan. 1974, p. 25).

We cannot have the attitude that it will go away or that the problem is everywhere else but in "our home" or "our valley." One of Satan's greatest traps is to lead us into believing that there is no problem or that whatever the problem is "It will never affect me or mine," or the, "I'm different than everyone else" syndrome.

When I hear statements such as these and I see people believing that music will not affect their spirit, II Nephi 28:21 comes to mind. "And others will he [Satan] pacify, and lull them away into carnal security, that they will say: All is well in Zion; yea, Zion prospereth, all is well—and thus the devil cheateth their souls, and leadeth them away carefully down to hell."

When we get the attitude that the music, or any other thing, will never affect us, then we are ripe to be lead "carefully down to hell." A short story about fishing on the Provo River illustrates this scripture wonderfully.

I have learned that if you want to catch the small ones, it is not that difficult. You don't have to be very careful. Simply follow a few basic procedures and nearly every time you go fishing, you can catch one or two. However, catching the big German Brown is a different story altogether. Being careful and patient are vital for success.

I love to put a fly or spinner on my line and work a few "secret" spots on the river, waiting for that "big one" to take what I offer. I know he's under there, watching my fly hit and skim across the water time after time, wondering if he dares to take it. He looks, swims a little closer, and seems to say, "I know it's probably from a local sporting goods store, but it looks so good I've got to have it!" I tease him more by working the fly back and forth until finally he says, "I know it's not good, but I've handled it before, I'm sure I can handle it again." Then boom! He hits it hard and starts to swim vigorously upstream. I let out a lot of line and let him think that he got away with it. Then when he feels like he succeeded, I carefully, very carefully, reel him in. He still appears to be swimming so well that it is difficult to believe he is in any danger.

Suddenly he sees my green boots. Reality strikes and he groans, "Oh no, if my parents knew I were here, they'd kill me!" With that statement he fights harder than ever before. He knows he is in trouble. I have him right where I want him. I continue to keep pressure on my line as I raise my pole above my head. With my free hand I reach for my net and carefully lower it under his fighting body.

The fish, knowing he is in trouble, fights diligently but by now his efforts are meaningless. Once he is in my net, I secure my pole beneath my arm and grab the fish carefully with one hand. I dislodge the fly, hold the fish up and say, "You really thought it was good didn't you! Sorry!" I then open my pouch, put him in it, and go on trying to catch another. He, on the other hand, hardly knows what has happened. He wonders, as he looks out of the small hole in my pouch, "How could this ever happen to me? This doesn't happen in real life. It only happens on soap operas!" He is caught, having been led carefully into my trap.

Are we sometimes like the fish with our music or videos? Satan can catch many people with little effort, just as I can the small fish. But when he goes after one who has been taught truth, he must be much more careful.

Are we being led away with our entertainment so carefully by the Master Deceiver, that we don't even know it is happening? Does some of the music of our day appear to be so good that we are being reeled in, hook, line and sinker?

Satan's music looks so good that we often cannot resist; we feel it is having little or no effect on us until he lowers the net, raises us up, and inserts his fingers through our "spiritual gills." He then opens his pouch, drops us in, and closes the lid. As we, like the fish, gaze out of the small hole, we finally realize that we are in trouble, that we have been deceived. Alma's words referring to Korihor, the anti-Christ, ring loudly in our ears: "And thus we see the end of him who perverteth the ways of the Lord; and thus we see that the devil will not support his chiildren at the last day, but doth speedily drag them down to hell," (Alma 30:60).

As we lie there, we begin wondering how our lives became so misled in such a short period of time. Thank God for the price that was paid. We are better off, by far, than the fish, for we have a loving Father who provided a way for us to change our course and rechart our lives, if we will but accept it.

Elder Neal A. Maxwell made this statement: "Now we are entering times wherein there will be for all of us as church members, in my judgment, some special challenges which will require of us that we follow the brethren. All the easy things that the church has had to do have been done. From now on, it's high adventure, and followership will be tested in some interesting ways," (Third Annual Religious Educators Symposium, Aug. 1979, p. 12).

With all that is going on in the media and the music industry, wouldn't you say that we are involved in "high adventure?" With the myriad of choices to be made concerning our music, it can plainly be seen that our followership is being and will be tested. The real question is, will we have the courage to follow our leaders and the scriptural teachings, or will we fall by the wayside? In my judgment, the times in which we are now living are different and perhaps more challenging than any other in the earth's history. We must have the wisdom to follow.

Elder Boyd K. Packer made a request concerning music. "I would recommend that you go through your record albums (may I also add tapes and videos), and set aside those records that promote the so-called new morality, the drug, or the hard rock culture. Such music ought not to belong to young people concerned about spiritual development.

"Why not go through your collection? Get rid of the worst of it. Keep just the best of it. Be selective in what you consume and what you produce. It becomes a part of you," (*Ensign*, Jan. 1974,

p. 27). Yes, a part of you, just like the onions became a part of my students.

If we have to go through our collections and make some changes then we must do it. We may not understand why at the present, but we must learn to follow a prophet. Our prophets have spoken. President Ezra Taft Benson in April, 1986 and then again in October of 1986 made the following statements concerning our entertainment and what Alma called the "lust of your eyes".

" 'The lusts of your eyes.' In our day, what does that expression mean? Movies, television programs, and video recordings that are both suggestive and lewd. Magazines and books that are obscene and pornographic.

We counsel you, young women (and men), not to pollute your minds with such degrading matter, for the mind through which this filth passes is never the same afterward. Don't see R-rated movies or vulgar videos or participate in any entertainment that is immoral, suggestive, or pornographic. And don't accept dates from young men who would take you to such entertainment . . . Instead, we encourage you to listen to uplifting music, both popular and classical, that builds the spirit. Learn some favorite hymns from our new hymnbook that build faith and spirituality. Attend dances where the music and the lighting and the dance movements are conducive to the Spirit. Watch those shows and entertainment that lift the spirit and promote clean thoughts and actions. Read books and magazines that do the same," (*Ensign*, Nov. 1986, p. 84).

President Benson makes the Lord's position very clear. Obviously it's not an easy thing to do and there are many who struggle with getting rid of that which appears to be so good and dear to the heart, yet inwardly is a spiritual onion. However, we must always remember that, "Someday when we look back on mortality, we will see that many of the things that seemed to matter so much at the moment will be seen not to have mattered at all. And the eternal things will be seen to have mattered even more than the most faithful of the saints imagined," (Neal A. Maxwell, *Even As I Am*, 1982, p. 104).

It is so easy at times, to place a high priority on items that, in the eternal perspective, are not of much importance at all. We live in a world that oftentimes puts emphasis on material possessions rather than principles such as home, family, and spirituality. We cannot get so caught up in the world that we forget who we really are.

The Savior, while giving the Sermon on the Mount, told us who we are when he said, "Ye are the light of the world. A city that is set on a hill cannot be hid. Neither do men light a candle, and put it under a bushel, but on a candlestick; and it giveth light unto all that are in the house.

" Let your light so shine before men, that they may see your good works, and glorify your Father which is in heaven," (Matthew 5:14-16).

President Spencer W. Kimball remarked: "You live in a time of wars and revolutions, yet the world will be revolutionized by the teaching of the gospel, which we must do . . . Women and men keeping the commandments of the Lord is the most revolutionary thing in the world," (*Church News*, March 13, 1979, p. 3).

In relation to today's youth being a "light unto the world," President Ezra Taft Benson, again bore testimony, "It is my conviction that the Lord has held back some of his choicest spirits to come forth in this age so they could help prepare for that second coming," (*Church News*, Feb. 24, 1976, pp. 9-10).

Can we not see that truth has been given to many so they can light the way for an ailing world? Wouldn't it be a tragedy if those that had the truth let their lights go out and the world lost its way, more so than it already has, because their music and other entertainment dimmed their spirits?

When it comes to making changes in our music and other forms of entertainment my mind turns to the story of Naaman and Elisha as told in II Kings 5. Naaman, a captian of the host of the king of Syria, was a great, honorable and courageous man. He was loved dearly by the king of Syria but suffered one major problem; he was a leper.

Fortunately for him, his wife had a "little maid" who knew of the prophet in Israel and communicated this message to the correct people in hopes of having this mighty man, Naaman, healed. When the king heard the story, he, because of his great love for

Naaman, insisted that Naaman go to Israel and be healed. Not only did he send 'ten talents of silver, two thousand pieces of gold, ten changes of raiment (clothing),' but he also sent a letter to the king of Israel explaining the problem and his desire to have his friend healed of leprosy.

When Naaman approached the king of Israel, the king was disturbed because of his inadequacies saying, "Am I God, to kill and to make alive, that this man doth send unto me to recover a man of his leprosy?" The king couldn't heal him and he knew it.

However Elisha the prophet heard about this confrontation and sent for Naaman. When Naaman arrived in all of his honor and glory, he stood at the door of the house of Elisha, expecting undoubtedly, a magnificent reception and honoring. To the contrary, the prophet sent a messenger with a very simple request to have Naaman, "Go and wash in Jordan seven times, and thy flesh shall come again to thee, and thou shalt be clean."

Naaman was furious at such a seemingly stupid request. As a result, he stormed away angry and upset, declaring that the rivers in Damascus were far superior to any in Israel. He was offended by the request of a prophet.

Then something very interesting happened. "And his servants came near, and spake unto him, and said, My father, if the prophet had bid thee do some great thing, wouldest thou not have done it? how much rather then, when he saith to thee, Wash, and be clean?

"Then went he down, and dipped himself seven times in Jordan, according to the saying of the man of God: and his flesh came again like unto the flesh of a little child, and he was clean," (II Kings 5:13-14).

He then returned to Elisha, gave thanks and praised the God of Israel. How much like Naaman are we when a man of God, a prophet, asks us to do something so simple as to go through our records, tapes and videos and "set aside" that which is inappropriate and hinders spiritual development? Do we feel that we know better than a prophet? Do we lack the faith to understand that obedience; or the lack of it, does affect our spiritual development?

I'm sure that if the prophet "bid thee to do some great thing," such as serve as a mission president, stake president, athletic star, movie star, bishop, general authority, or millionaire, "wouldest thou not have done it?"

If we are so willing to do the "great things," what about doing the simple things, such as paying tithing, serving missions, working on the welfare farm, praying, or even getting rid of inappropriate music.

Remember, when Naaman repented and followed the "man of God," his leprosy was healed and he was blessed. The Lord wants to "heal" and bless our lives if we but learn to follow and be obedient. He has told us, "I, the Lord, am bound when ye do what I say; but when ye do not what I say, ye have no promise," (D&C 82:10).

Hopefully in this matter of music, and other forms of entertainment, it will not be said of you or me as it was the young rich man who approached Jesus with a question of what he had to do to gain eternal life. Jesus replied: "Keep the commandments." The young man inquired which commandments he should keep, and Jesus answered, quoting the ten commandments, "The young man saith unto him, All these have I kept from my youth up: what lack I yet?

"Jesus said unto him, . . . go and sell that thou hast, . . . and come and follow me . . .

"But when the young man heard that saying, he went away sorrowful: for he had great possessions," (Matthew 19:16-22).

Wouldn't it be tragic if anyone were to say, "I'm sorry Lord, I can't follow what thou hast asked of me concerning music, because I just have too much money invested in inappropriate tapes and records, and it would simply cost too much to weed out my collection."

Hopefully all people everywhere will have the wisdom and the courage to "come listen to a prophet's voice."

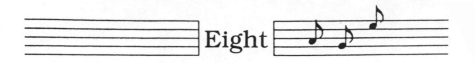 

# Eight

# A Solution

In August 1985 I met a young man who changed my perceptions of music and my desire to do good with it. I was in the process of finishing graduate school when one of my fellow students asked me about my speaking and writing concerning music.

As we discussed some of the research I had done he mentioned that he knew a young man from Colorado who had been influenced by music tremendously. In fact he said that the boy and his parents were staying at one of the local dorms while going to summer school. He asked if I would like to meet the boy. Of course, I told him I would be extremely interested. Little did I know then what a profound effect Luke Jones would have in my life.

As we walked through the door I was approached by a young boy just under six years of age that was extremely scarred on his head, arms, and hands. Upon seeing me he stretched forth his hand to meet me and said, "Hello mister. My name is Luke Jones. What's yours?" I told him my name and the man who had brought me told Luke why I had come. He said, "That's great. I gotta go play with my friends. See ya later. Have a wonderful day."

I was shocked. I was set back. I couldn't believe the outgoing manner of such a young boy. After being introduced to Luke's parents, they proceeded to show me a video about his life and accomplishments. They told me he was part of the Miracle Telethon and the reason why Luke was in his current condition. Before they told me the story of Luke's accident and how he received his scars, they informed me that music was one of the greatest influences in Luke's life. When he was frustrated or overly excited he would sing. The singing would calm him down and his frustrations would flee. He also struggled at times, with recalling material he had learned, but when listening to or playing music on the piano, his recall significantly increased.

It was amazing that music could play such a vital role in the life of someone so young. But as the story unfolded it became much more clear how powerful and wonderful good wholesome music is in each of our lives and why it is so vital that we have it.

When Luke was 1 1/2 he had a tragic accident while sitting on the edge of his mother's washing machine. A load of wash had just been placed in the washer, when Luke's mother was called to take care of other sick children. In her haste, she momentarily forgot about Luke sitting on the washing machine. Immediately, upon realizing she had left Luke in a dangerous position, she ran back to the wash room. To her horror she saw that Luke had fallen head first into the washing machine. She instinctively removed him and administered first aid trying to revive him and save his life. When the ambulance finally arrived Luke was rushed to the local hospital.

He spent four months in intensive care having suffered three major injuries. Sixty percent of his little body had been burned by the scalding water. He had all but drowned, as well as suffering severe head injuries from being hit with the paddles of the washer. Very few people thought that Luke would live. But he did. After leaving the hospital he wore a rubber mask and hat for 18 months to cover his severe scarring.

Finally, when his mother felt it was time for Luke to now interact with other children, both parents had a great fear that he would have a very difficult time adjusting and that the other children would have a difficult time adjusting to him and his new appearance.

Luke's mother served at the time as Primary president. She decided to discuss Luke's situation with his Sunbeam teacher. With great confidence in the teacher this valiant mother asked if the teacher would take special care of Luke and help him adjust to this very difficult time in his life.

When Luke entered the Primary class for the first time, his appearance particularly frightened one little girl. She screamed with fear and started into hysterics. She would not stop. The teacher, in desperation, trying to calm the girl down and also trying to assure the other class members that everything was under control, had Luke come to the front of the class and pull up his rubber mask. She calmly said, "Now see boys and girls, Luke is a real boy. He's just like you." The other children were so intrigued by what they saw underneath the mask that they rushed towards Luke in order to get a closer look. This sudden rush of movement and attention frightened Luke terribly. The children pressed upon him trying to see what was under his covering, while the hysterical little girl continued her screaming in a distant corner.

Luke began to panic. The only way he knew to calm down his fear and frustration was to do what he had always done. Sing. With a quivering voice this sweet little boy began to sing "I Am A Child of God" in his moment of need and trial. The teacher told the mother that the class joined in and finished singing this beautiful prayer unto God. The music so soothed the class that by the end of the meeting Luke was coloring in a book with the little girl who had been so hysterical. The song from a little boy's heart, his plea to God for help, his remembering who he was and calling upon God in his own way through music, caused a calmness and peace to come upon that room and each individual. It also was an answer to his parents prayers that Luke could make it throughout his life. This wonderful experience brought peace and joy to all who were involved in it. Oh, that each of us could learn from little Luke Jones.

Music when used in its proper way can bring peace and comfort and joy. Is beautiful music an answer to many a parent's prayer? Could the problem with some of the music our young people are listening to be the source or the root of their problems? We must understand that as Luke was so important to his parents and that music was able to bless his life, so each of our children and each one of us is important to our Father in Heaven.

"Remember the worth of souls is great in the sight of God," (D&C 18:10). Every single soul is precious to Him. We must never forget this while dealing with music. We cannot rest until each of our Father's sheep is brought safely into the arms of the true Shepherd. Just one young man or woman does make a difference and I for one do not like to see one of them, regardless of their problems, standing on the outside wondering how to weather the storms of life. We cannot afford to lose one of our youth to the powers of inappropriate music.

Horace Mann made this statement at the dedication of a boy's home. "If all the work and energy and money put into the endeavor saved but one boy it would be worth it." He was then questioned by someone as being insincere and becoming too oratorical. "Oh yes, I meant it," Horace Mann insisted. "It would have all been worth it if the one were my son." Again we cannot stop until all people are brought within the influence of the Master.

I realize that many people have perhaps already gone beyond the feeling point, having rejected all the gospel offers. Yet we must not cease trying to bring them back. Too often we forget the most important factor in dealing with music, or any other difficult issue, is that people who are of the ultimate worth.

People often comment to me that if they interpret the 13th Article of Faith correctly, and Moroni 7, and Elder Packer's teachings, they would never be able to listen to any music in the category of "popular." I disagree. I often tune my radio to what I judge to be acceptable popular music. I simply reserve the right to change stations if an inappropriate song comes on.

There are better ways to solve the problems of choosing between the musical apples and onions of our day. As in all decisions of discernment, the Spirit must become our guide. This means that we must use wisdom and love in guiding those who struggle with these decisions. Alma's words to his son Shiblon are appropriate. "Use boldness, but not overbearance; and also see that ye bridle all your passions, that ye may be filled with love," (Alma 38:12).

We must be bold, but never "overbearing." In our counseling we must be filled with love, and we must allow people to do things of their own free will and choice, but we cannot be afraid of our children or afraid that they might get angry or run away. Child development experts suggest that parents take charge. They must take the lead and show the way for their children, (*U.S. News and World Report*, Oct. 8, 1985, p. 54).

President Eisenhower understood this principle. To illustrate it, he would, in a Cabinet meeting, lay a long piece of string down on the table. Then he would pick up one end of the string and try to push it forward. It would always become entangled. Then he would pull the string and it followed freely.

Somehow if we can gently lead, if we can pull rather than push people along— teaching by example, love and patience—perhaps many will follow.

What will happen in our homes when posters of inappropriate artists go up on bedroom walls, when styles shift to dramatic clothing and hairstyles, when school grades drop and the sweet nature of our child turns irritable. How will we handle such a situation? Here is where I believe we need to take charge, but we must do it in an appropriate way. Hopefully no parent or guardian would be unwise enough to go into a young person's room and destroy their record albums and tapes or tear down everything on the wall without consulting with the child first. We must reason together. We must begin to ask questions as to why certain drastic changes in behavior are taking place.

Robert Coles, a Harvard child psychiatrist has said, "If strong family or church life is absent, what other moral influences are there?" He suggests that some of these vast behavorial changes are signals that adults should notice when entertainment threatens emotional health, (Ibid, p. 54).

Darlyne Pettinicchio, co-founder of Back in Control Training Center in Fullerton, California, suggests that music is the number one indicator of emotional problems. She says the troubled kids will be totally absorbed in either heavy metal or punk music. Then she suggests that a rebellious stage sets in. Some even become physically violent and very aggressive, responding to their parents with the "you can't tell me what to do" attitude. Hairstyles change drastically and their clothing becomes very dark. She and other experts suggest that in enforcing rules for school attendance and household chores are vital and, if necessary, there may even be a ban on certain types of music. She does suggest that, yes, they may get upset but you have to give clear direct commands and signals. However, we must be extremely wise and intelligent in how we go about this process, (Ibid, p. 54).

Dr. Bruno Bettelheim, who taught at the University of Chicago for many years and is an internationally known child psychologist, suggests that if a child is addicted to a certain kind of music or to a certain musical group, that means there is a gap in his life he is trying to fill.

Many teenagers turn up their stereos full volume to blast other thoughts out of their heads. It is a way of getting away from troubling feelings or to fill a void. It's similar to an addiction to drugs. People become addicted not because drugs are around but because of emptiness. If everything in a young person's life is in order then the media will have very little influence.

Dr. Bettelheim goes on to suggest that a teenager has to make judgments based on quality but he cannot do that by himself. He needs help and to provide it parents must have good judgment themselves. If they watch trash or listen to trash how are they going to help a child develop good judgment? Usually whatever is the most popular entertainment of the time is blamed for everything, but much in the media can be made constructive if parents take an interest, (*U.S. News & World Report*, Oct. 28, 1985, p. 55).

As Latter-day Saints we must be holding regular, quality Family Home Evenings on the subject. Issues of music could be regularly mentioned in family prayers and scripture study. If we have patient faith the Lord will aid us. If we teach our children diligently I believe he will keep his promises and cause that "his grace shall attend you." He will bless us but not when we overreact in a fit of anger or impatience.

The best advice I have ever heard on handling the subject is the analogy of a young child picking up a sharp object. Sometimes a foolish adult will grab for it, frightened for the safety of the child. Instinctively, the child may grip it more tightly and perhaps injure himself or injure the parent as he pulls away. The wise parent will trade him for it some equally appealing, but harmless, object given in exchange so that he lets go willingly and without tears.

We must keep that in mind when we have a problem with young people and their music. To change it may take some time and require a great deal of inspiration.

Changing people requires, "persuasion, by long-suffering, by gentleness and meekness, and by love unfeigned; By kindness," (D&C 121:41-42). We must provide constructive and interesting alternatives. We must keep in mind the marvelous injunction that "to tell is to preach, to ask is to teach."

The question arises then, if our young people and adults change their music habits, with what do they replace their former tastes? Perhaps the question can be answered with a question. Why aren't more Latter-day Saints composing and producing music that is appropriate. President Heber J. Grant in a way implied that same question: "I wish that as far as possible we would get into the habit of singing our own music, that is, music composed by our own people, (April Conference Report, 1934).

One of the major solutions to the musical dilemma, in my opinion, is to flood the market with wholesome, edifying music. Why should we sit back idly and allow the adversary nearly total control of this most powerful medium? We must, as a people contribute more to what today's youth, as well as adults, listen to, by writing, composing and producing music that meets the Lord's approval.

Orson F. Whitney thought this possible. "We shall yet have Miltons and Shakespeares of our own. God's ammunition is not exhausted. His highest spirits are held in reserve for the latter times. In God's name and by his help we will build up a literature whose tops will touch the heaven, though its foundation may now be low on the earth," (Boyd K. Packer, "The Arts and the Spirit of the Lord," BYU 12-Stake Fireside, Feb. 1, 1976, p. 3).

I believe we shall not only have Miltons and Shakespeares, but that we will have Beethovens and Bachs as well. We must believe in ourselves and have hope in our abilities. We must seek to live clean lives in order to receive the inspiration necessary to compose music that will not only be appealing to our people but edifying as well. We must always remember that "the brightest lights shine from the cleanest instruments."

Some Latter-day Saints have taken the challenge and are producing and performing wonderful, inspiring music. To those I say, thank you for enriching my life and satisfying the needs of the young people. Thank you for making the music decision easier and more rewarding. However, we need many more Latter-day Saints to make this much needed contribution in the vital area of music.

Perhaps one reason our people do not produce more good music is that we as a people do not seek eagerly enough the spirit to guide our pens but rather seek to please the world. We have been instructed well in this matter: "It is a mistake to assume that one can follow the ways of the world and then somehow, in a moment of intruded inspiration, compose a great anthem of the Restoration; or in a moment of singular inspiration paint the great painting. When it is done, it will be done by one who has yearned and tried and longed fervently to do it; not by one who has condescended to do it. It will take quite as much preparation and work as any masterpiece and a different kind of inspiration," (Ibid, p. 7).

As was stated earlier, perhaps the greatest hymns and anthems may not yet have been composed. When they are produced, who will produce them? "They will be produced by those who are the most inspired among us," (Ibid, p. 10). Note that the last line did not say the most "famous," or the most "talented," but the most "inspired"—by those who have sought not only to communicate the will of the Lord but have lived according to His mind and will.

Too often, perhaps, we do not achieve all we could in using our musical talents because we worry about pleasing the world rather than God, (see Gal. 5:16-17)

There is as much responsibility on the performer as there is on the listener, (see D&C 50:17-22). If we could bear equal responsibility, we would accomplish much in the way of a solution to our "music problem."

President Joseph Fielding Smith remarked on the principle of singleness of purpose. "Now if you understand the gospel of Jesus Christ, it will make you free. If your softball, your volleyball, your basketball, your footracing, your dancing, and other entertainment (music), are devoid of the spirit of the Lord, they will be of no value to you . . . Do everything with an eye single unto the glory of God, and let us teach to build up and strengthen ourselves and the Church of Jesus Christ of Latter-Day Saints," (*Take Heed Yourself*, p. 86).

If we could do this, I am confident that our music and other arts would become a standard to the good people of the world.

In summary, these are some of the basic keys to a solution:

1. Take charge of the situation; teach, exhort, expound.
2. Provide creative, interesting alternatives.
3. Be wise in how we go about helping our young people with their music.
4. Follow the teachings of the scriptures and of the living prophets in the standards they set for choosing.
5. Flood the market with that which is good.
6. Seek the Spirit of the Lord in all we do.

It is also suggested that all people who desire to influence people for good and who wish to nurture and perfect their music abilities have the courage to do just that! Such individuals should not become bogged down in the unworthy music of our day. They should have faith in God and in themselves. Each of us is a son or daughter of God, and we have within us the abilities to become instruments in God's hands to achieve that which is good.

I have faith that this can be done. We can light a light for all the world to follow in the ever growing darkness if each of us will choose to follow the Lord in our choices in music, as well as in all our pursuits in life.

I once heard a statement at a BYU stake conference that I have never forgotten. "Following the prophet is not always easy, but it is always right." I have come to know that truer words were never spoken. "For only if we are unafraid of truth will we ever find it."

My friends, the decision is yours. Each person must decide for himself if he will listen to or produce musical "apples" or "onions."

This decision is not an easy one. However, our decisions concerning our entertainment can influence us for the rest of our lives. As Robert Frost wrote, "Two roads diverged in a wood, and I, I took the one less traveled by, and that has made all the difference," (*American Literature*, "Tradition and Innovation," p. 2859).